Posting the Word

Chris Harris and the Story of
Life Light Home Study Courses

— CHRIS HARRIS —

Sacristy
Press

Sacristy Press
PO Box 612, Durham, DH1 9HT

www.sacristy.co.uk

First published in 2022 by Sacristy Press, Durham

Sacristy Limited, registered in England & Wales, number 7565667

British Library Cataloguing-in-Publication Data
A catalogue record for the book is available from the British Library

ISBN 978-1-78959-204-7

This book is dedicated to
Josh, Lauren, Lilly and Alice

Contents

Acknowledgements . . . . **v**
Preface . . . . **vi**

Part I. Life Light: The Roots **1**
Chapter 1. What I Woke up To 3
Chapter 2. Towards Priesthood during the 1950s 13
Chapter 3. Living Through the Second Vatican Council 31
Chapter 4. From Lumen Vitae to Life Light 43
Chapter 5. Hawkstone Hall Correspondence Courses 56

Part II. Life Light: The Flowering and Growth **71**
Chapter 6. The Birth of Life Light 73
Chapter 7. Working with St Mary's 83
Chapter 8. Spirituality—from the Cloister to the Hearth 98
Chapter 9. Helping Out All Round 117
Chapter 10. The Catholic Certificate in Religious Studies 132
Chapter 11. Domestic Bliss 147
Chapter 12. Tranquillity Tested and Restored 160
Chapter 13. Sharing a Resource 167

Post-word **187**
Appendix I. List of Modules **190**
Appendix II. Annual Enrolments, 1974–2021 . . . . **191**
Notes **192**

Acknowledgements

To Natalie K. Watson and Susan Hibbins for much assistance in the preparation of this text.

To the very many from whom I have received much help, kindness, spiritual and material help along my way.

In particular, I am grateful to members of the Congregation of the Most Holy Redeemer, the Redemptorists, who nurtured my spiritual life as an adolescent parishioner of Erdington Abbey, provided me with an experience of religious life for a quarter of a century, enabled both my pre- and post-Vatican II theological education, introduced me to distance learning as a seminarian and, crucially, made it possible for Hawkstone Hall Correspondence Courses to morph into Life Light Home Study Courses.

Preface

Christ is fading from our daily lives. What do you make of this?

Have you ever thought of doing something about it?

Posting the Word tells the story of how one Catholic couple actually did something about it. Heather and I worked together throughout our married lives to develop a simple way of communicating knowledge and insights about the Bible, Tradition and Christian practice to men and women of our time.

"Life Light Home Study Courses" has been our life's work. Nearly half a century old, and with an interesting story, Life Light has delivered home study tuition to over 13,000 students from many walks of life, many different countries and with a wide range of age, aptitude and ability.

The story began long before we married. I think that many will find much of interest in this story, especially if they have been involved with the same areas of life as I have been: the Church, the spiritual lives of lay Christians, religious education in schools and, notably, adult religious education. I have dedicated most of my life to adult religious education and in particular to answering this question: "How may we meaningfully speak to the modern adult about God?"

These pages also relate how the many changes to church life, science and theology affected one person as I passed through religious life, priesthood, teaching, marriage and family life. During this time my life was torpedoed periodically by deep doubts about the existence of God. I have written in some detail about these doubts, in particular about how I emerged from them, in the hope that my fellow doubters may find this helpful.

In addition, I have described life's common joys and challenges, and have tried to bring out some of their spiritual dimensions, in the hope that my experiences will resonate with others.

Our course participants have fed us constantly with inspiration drawn from accounts of their diverse experiences. I will share some of this resource in the concluding chapter.

PART I

Life Light: The Roots

Part I covers my background, my early days; my adolescence and life experiences up to my forties. I shall use my diaries, my passport back to a world that has now largely passed into oblivion—the Catholic parish ghetto of World War II days, the hothouse atmosphere of the 1950s noviciates and the academic claustrophobia of the pre-Vatican II seminary.

My diaries enable me to make detailed contact with how I felt at each and every stage of the dramatic changes which challenged the Church during the 1960s and 70s, and especially during the period of the Second Vatican Council. They also make it possible to revisit my innermost thoughts as I struggled with deep problems of faith and sought ways out of my many difficulties. I will share with you my innermost thoughts as I worked my way through the painful process of laicization.

Towards the end of Part I I recount the precise point at which the inspiration for Life Light occurred and the somewhat tortuous road that I trod on the way to bringing it to the full light of day.

1

What I Woke up To

Christmas Eve 1934 was unlike any other in our family. My two brothers, John and Tony, were full of curious expectation as they awaited their baby sister. She was keeping them waiting; she should have arrived on 8 December. When I did put in my appearance, on the 24th, Tony thought it only right for a responsible four-year-old to go upstairs and tell his mother that "my little sister has arrived—but she's a boy!"

I was named after my Uncle Chris. He was at the time a seminarian at Hawkstone Hall in Shropshire, preparing for the priesthood. Perhaps my mother's sub-conscious hope in so naming me was that I too might one day be a priest. (Well . . . if he can't be a girl, he might as well be the next best thing—a priest!)

I woke up to find myself in a very Catholic family. How did this come about?

My great-grandfather Joseph Harris (born c.1830) came to Birmingham from Wales in the mid-nineteenth century at a time when the city was expanding rapidly with new residents arriving from all sides. Joseph was a Welsh Presbyterian. One day he became conscious of an old lady who passed by his house every morning, rain or shine. Out of curiosity on one occasion he followed her. He discovered that she made this daily journey so as to attend Mass at the local Catholic church. This was the first stage of his next journey of faith. He was eventually received into the Catholic Church.

He married Catherine Davies (1833–91), who was also a Catholic, and together they ran a china shop in Lichfield Road, Aston. They finally settled in the Abbey parish in Erdington. The Benedictine community of Weingarten in Germany had been expelled during the anti-clericalist Kulturkampf era under Otto von Bismarck (1815–98) and by 1876 had built a new Abbey in Erdington, attached to the already existing church of St Thomas and St Edmund, founded by Father Daniel Haigh. Joseph's family became very attached to the community, and his daughters, Teresa, Rita and May, were particularly devoted to it. May actually bequeathed to them six small cottages in Station Road which skirted the Abbey grounds.

Then there was "Church Emma". Emma Boreman (1825–1911), a cousin of Catherine Davies who had been orphaned at an early age, came from London to live with the family in Erdington. She became housekeeper to Father Haigh from 1850 and, for a time, lived an anchorite existence in the Angelus tower near the church porch, hence "Church Emma". She stayed there and assisted the Benedictine monks who were always very kind to her—especially in her old age when she moved back into the family. She enjoyed something of a reputation of a saint. After her death in 1911, the family and the local Dominican Sisters were careful to collect some of her little bits and pieces (notably a famous christening shawl) in the firm expectation of her one day being canonized!

Another orphaned cousin of Catherine was Elizabeth Davies. Aged twenty, she was recommended by Dom Leo Wulfe of the Abbey community to the Benedictine Sisters at Princethorpe in Warwickshire, where she became Sister Mildred OSB (1861–1956). As a young boy I remember frequently being taken, as a special family treat, to see Sister Mildred. I did not know how great a part Princethorpe would play at a later stage in my life (see Chapter 11)!

Joseph and Catherine had many children, the youngest son of whom was my own grandfather, Vincent. They were a pious family. Joseph's family prized being friends with the clergy, among whom were Father Dominic Barberi (1772–1849), the Passionist priest who received St John Henry Newman into the Catholic Church, Canon Withers (a frequent visitor from Oscott College, the local diocesan seminary) and several members of the Abbey community—both Benedictines and, after 1922, Redemptorists.

Founded by St Alphonsus de Liguori in 1749 near Naples in Italy, the Congregation of the Most Holy Redeemer (CSSR), or "Redemptorists", arrived in England in 1843, where they quickly flourished. After the end of World War I in 1918, they needed more spacious accommodation for their seminarians. At the same time, the Erdington German monks were looking to return to their homeland since experiencing difficulties during the war. The transfer of Erdington Abbey from the monks to the Redemptorists solved both problems.

My own father, also called Vincent, married Marie Lord, eldest daughter of Herbert and Gertrude Lord. Gertrude wore herself out doing charitable work within the Abbey parish. One of the things she organized was to put together a christening kit. This was always at the ready for whenever she heard of an unbaptized child in danger of death. In line with the preaching of the monks, she wanted to save babies from eternal misery. On her premature deathbed in 1937, she made my mother promise that one of her boys would become a priest. She herself, again following frequent preaching by the clergy, would dearly have loved to have had a son a priest. Unfortunately, her only son died in infancy.

My young years

It was within the setting of the Erdington Abbey Redemptorist parish that I spent my early years (1934–51). At the tender age of five, I was put into a cassock and surplice and instructed how to perform the office of boat-bearer at Benediction, carrying the "boat" that contained the incense grains to be used in the thurible at High Mass and Benediction. Within twelve months I was serving Mass daily, carefully enunciating "*Ad Deum qui laetificat juventutem meam . . .* " (without the faintest idea what all this actually meant!). This was 1941, the second year of World War II. Occasionally I would set off cycling to the Abbey before the "all clear" had been sounded after the frequent air raids of that year. (This was "Warsaw Concerto" territory, as distinct from *The Sound of Music*![1]) On these occasions my mother told me to cycle via the Post Office (where there was an air raid shelter). If bombs started falling before I reached that point, I was to go down the shelter. Beyond that point I was to make for the Abbey. If I got killed, I would go straight to heaven! Otherwise, my guardian angel (to whom she had an enormous devotion) would see me all right (cf. Matthew 18:10).

On a Sunday it was common for many parishioners to go to the Abbey Church three times: early morning Mass and Communion, High Mass at

11 am and Rosary–Sermon–Benediction at 6.30 pm. I served in various capacities in all three for ten years. I naturally mimicked the priests I served and increasingly hero-worshipped them. I "said Mass" in my bedroom. Mum encouraged me in this and lovingly handmade an alb, stole and chasuble.

I soaked up unquestioningly the small, cosy world that I found myself in. Not just the religious aspect, but everything else too. I believed the family legends that were retold at family meals and which grew exponentially in the telling. A feature of these was the family boasting of all the inventions and gadgets that the family had (or should have) patented. I believed that Great-grandfather Joseph had invented roller skates, and that Grandad Lord (on my mother's side) had played a part in first putting names in rock, and that his father was at school in Nottinghamshire with Jesse Boot (the founder of Boots the Chemist). We were told how Joseph one day witnessed a young mother trip and lose control of her pram and baby on the sharp inclined pavement of New Town Row in central Birmingham. He immediately returned home, went to his workshop and designed a pram that would come to a halt if the mother let go of the handle. Birmingham, the "City of a thousand and one trades", could indeed boast of much inventiveness, from James Watt (1736–1819) and his steam engine to John Dedicoat and his bicycle bell in 1877, and hundreds of gadgets besides. Inventiveness mixed with the thick smoke of Birmingham pubs. The ethos of the time and place was "You got a problem? I can fix that!" It was only very much later that I learned to my utter amazement that roller skates were in fact invented by another Brummie, William Brown. Nevertheless, the handing down of family legends, whether true or not, promoted inventiveness and educated us in an informal way to glimpse what we too might achieve.

The world to which I had awoken was indeed cosy and small. Living in the Abbey parish had its ghetto-like aspects. We were not allowed to play with boys and girls who were not Catholics. (I myself was not allowed to play with girls of *any* description!) We received all our education within Catholic primary and secondary schools. My mother, in this pre-supermarket age, did all her shopping as far as possible at shops run by Catholics. We had a Catholic doctor, Catholic dentist, Catholic butcher etc. Our social life was catered for by clubs and societies set up by the Abbey: the Youth Club, Women's Guild and various spiritual groups like the Children of Mary. After Sunday evening Benediction most weeks there was a "social" in the Abbey Hall, a handsome purpose-built edifice which accommodated concerts, dances, wedding receptions and much else. And, of course, there was a Catholic cemetery. The average parishioner could, and did, find most of his/her needs satisfied within the Catholic circle of priests and parishioners.

How did the ghetto mentality come about?

From the time of the Reformation in the sixteenth century, Catholics had become increasingly marginalized by English society as a whole. Apart from the periods of open persecution, there was a general feeling after the Gunpowder Plot (1605) that Catholics were not fully-fledged Brits and that they owed too much allegiance to the pope in Rome. The Five Mile Act (1665) prevented Catholic priests from coming within five miles of any corporate town. The Gordon Riots of 1780, which reacted against the Catholic Relief Act of 1778, made Catholics apprehensive of their non-Catholic neighbours for a long time. One of Church Emma's duties was to warn the Abbey parishioners by ringing the Angelus bell if any angry crowds approached Erdington Abbey. From the 1840s, the parish welcomed hundreds of families from Ireland, especially after the potato famine of 1845. These new parishioners had already experienced marginalization in their own homeland. They found the mindset of their new fellow parishioners not at all unfamiliar. The ethos of marginalization was thereby intensified.

A further component of this ghetto mentality was inspired by nineteenth-century events in the Vatican. The annexation by 1870 of the Papal States by the youthful Italian state made Pope Pius IX and others feel that the Church itself had become marginalized. The ensuing First Vatican Council (1870) reacted with its definition of papal supremacy and infallibility. Catholics worldwide were thereafter inclined to be surer of themselves, to be "triumphalist", and to hold church teaching as sound and certain in every detail. We frequently sang with gusto the convert-poet Aubrey de Vere's (1814–1902) hymn of praise to the

Catholic Church, "Who is she that stands triumphant, Rock in strength, upon the Rock? Hers the kingdom, hers the sceptre; fall, ye nations, at her feet." This same spirit was evident in the papal bull *Apostolicae curae* of 1896 which declared Anglican Orders to be "absolutely null and utterly void". Everything was clear-cut and absolutely certain—black and white. God was in his heaven above keeping a check on me 24/7, intervening favourably in response to prayers and punishing me when I did something wrong.

I grew up influenced greatly by these various circumambient forces felt in our home, school and parish—but especially in the sermons preached by the members of the Abbey community whom I greatly admired. If I ever thought about such things, I would prize the Catholic Church as the sole true Church, with non-Catholics heading for an eternity in Hell.

I recall one particularly eloquent and effective Sunday evening sermon preached on the conversion of England. I would have been about seven years of age. With the benefit of hindsight, it was full of the spirit of the last three paragraphs, concluding with a final haranguing challenge to *do something* about converting our neighbours. I cycled home, went to my bedroom and wondered how to convert England. I took out my brother Tony's school atlas of the British Isles and surveyed the problem. Ah yes . . . easy!

I zoomed in on Cornwall. I would go to the first house in Land's End. I would knock on the door and convert the person inside. Shouldn't take long—about fifteen minutes should suffice. Then I would go next door and do the same. I would then gradually work my way up the country.

Then I fell asleep.

My second confession

The Abbey Primary School was ably directed by the Dominican Sisters from St Agnes' Convent located within the parish. I attended this school during the war years. On reflection, I think that the Sisters and their lay assistants performed very well in the circumstances, making use of the most up-to-date insights of educationalists of the period in terms of teaching numeracy and literacy.

It was Sister Bernard who prepared us for First Confession and First Holy Communion. St Pius X (1835–1914) had brought forward to ages seven or eight the point at which Catholics could start receiving Holy Communion. Since Confession and Communion were traditionally so stringently bracketed together, this change logically meant that children began engaging in the Sacrament of Reconciliation at an age earlier than ever before in Christian history.

Sister prepared us well for First Confession. We knew what to tell the priest at our first confession and how to go about it. We were to take the Ten Commandments (from the *Simple Prayer Book*) as a basis for our examination of conscience.

"How often should we go to Confession, please, Sister?" I asked.

"You serve on the altar. You must go every week."

"But if I've done nothing during the week?"

"You, Chris Harris, will *always* have done something. 'The just man falls seven times a day'" (a then common misquotation of Proverbs 24:16).

None of us in our class of thirty had any problems with our First Confession. We dutifully lined up in the pews by the four confessionals in the Abbey church. Four Redemptorist priests listened to the "crimes" each of us had committed over our first seven years and duly gave us absolution.

My own problem arose in connection with that second confession a week later. I returned to church for the weekly Saturday confession times, duly took out my *Simple Prayer Book*, turned to the list of the Ten Commandments and mentally ticked off those which I thought I had contravened. First—no. Second—no. Third—no. Fourth—no. Fifth—no. Sixth—don't know what that is. Seventh—no. Eighth—no. Ninth—no. Tenth—no.

So . . . in I went to make my second confession to Father Holloway.

"Please, Father, give me your blessing for I have sinned. It is one week since my last confession. I was horrid to my brother. And I committed adultery."

"How many times?"

"Forty-eight!"

As far as I recall Father Holloway gave me three Hail Marys.

In later years, when composing the Life Light module on the Sacraments, this childhood experience fed into the approach I took.

Growing up

From the Abbey school I passed in 1945 to St Philip's Grammar School (SPGS) in Edgbaston. St John Henry Newman (1801–90) founded the famous Oratory School here in 1859 as a Catholic alternative to Eton College. The Oratory School subsequently moved to its current location in Pangbourne, near Reading, leaving the Edgbaston school premises available for the setting up of St Philip's Grammar School in 1887. Among the many famous old boys are Eamon Duffy (Professor of Church History at Cambridge), Paul Beard (leader of the BBC Symphony Orchestra), Field Marshal Viscount Bill Slim (hero of two world wars) and (for a time) J. R. R. Tolkien (author of *The Hobbit* and *Lord of the Rings*). All the male members of our family attended St Philip's: my father, my elder brothers John and Tony and myself. Tony was already at the school when I started there.

The spirit of Newman pervaded the school. Of particular significance was the promotion of the *lay* Catholic within the Church. All but two of the teaching staff were lay, including the headmaster, T. J. Larkin. In his *Idea of a University*, Newman wrote: "I want a laity . . . men who know what they hold and what they do not, who know their creed so well that they can give an account of it, who know so much history that they can defend it." This spirit was to stand a number of us SPGS boys in good stead in the Vatican II years; for example, when *Gaudium et spes* 62 would re-echo this quotation from Newman.

I owe much to St Philip's—even though I did not appreciate it at the time. The majority of the teachers were Catholic. Oratorian Fathers Louis Brodeur and Geoffrey Walmsley took the "Doctrine" classes (as they were then labelled) and the other staff members left Catholicity to them. Catholicity very rarely came explicitly into their teaching of Maths, Science, English, and so on; rather, it was implicit throughout everything that happened. On one occasion, when I was having doubts about the existence of God, I spotted Mr Smith, my Physics teacher, going to Communion during a school Mass. I remember being very affected by this sight. I thought to myself: "If *he*, a science teacher, thinks all this makes sense, then I should too!"

My brother Tony took his School Certificate in 1947. In August of that year, he joined the Redemptorist noviciate in Kinnoull, Perth, Scotland. The following year he was professed and started his seminary course at Hawkstone Hall in Shropshire. My mother was ecstatic.

From this point, I became a rather serious adolescent. I began to keep a diary. I would take a train from Erdington to Lichfield and then walk the country lanes in deep thought. Despite entering fully into all the myriad features of a fervent Catholic life, every now and again with the onset of puberty I began to wonder whether there really was, after all, a God. My problem was that I liked all the peripherals—serving daily Mass, parish life, saying my prayers—but *if* there was no God, then the whole edifice collapsed. Jesus, doubtless a good man, would have been mistaken. The Church he founded became foundationless. The "Penny Catechism" would not be worth a penny at all. Usually my doubts would soon pass, often with the next Mass I served, but I was prone to such doubts repeatedly for several decades.

In 1950, during the first two weeks after Easter, the Guild of St Stephen (the Altar Servers' Guild) organized a national pilgrimage to Rome. Although I was only fifteen, Mum and Dad were comfortable with my decision to join this pilgrimage. They trusted the priest-pilgrims one hundred per cent: and then of course our guardian angels could probably get their passports too!

We numbered about fifty. We set off from London's Victoria Station on the boat train to Newhaven and crossed to Dieppe. Always a train enthusiast myself, I really enjoyed my first trips on the SNCF to Paris and on the night train from the Gare de Lyon to Rome. We were lodged in the Vatican itself, in the Casa Santa Marta, to the left of St Peter's Basilica as one approaches from the Piazza. These premises later became the apartments of the present Pope Francis, who decided against the splendour and luxury of the traditional Papal Apartments.

We servers were well looked after, notably by Father Gerard Harrison SCJ who organized the details of several of our sightseeing trips to the Catacombs, Basilicas, Sistine Chapel and elsewhere. We took part in a general Papal Audience with Pius XII. He gave our group a special mention. I took a private trip to Via Merulana, the General House of the Redemptorists, to call on Father Joseph Hanton, a friend of the family who was studying in Rome at the time.

My diary records how, from this time forward, I became increasingly passionate in my desire to become a Redemptorist priest and to follow Tony to St Mary's, Kinnoull. At 6.30 each morning, before commuting to St Philip's, I served Father Peter Wilson, headmaster of the Redemptorist Junior Seminary, now housed within the Abbey. In line with my mathematical approach to spirituality, I began to keep count of the number of Masses I "heard" (as well as the total days of Indulgence I had gained for the souls in Purgatory). By the end of 1951, I had taken part in 434 Masses that year!

I applied on 6 January 1951 to the Provincial, Father Wilfrid Hughes, to be admitted to the postulancy and noviciate. A favourable reply arrived back on 23 January. I was taken into Burton's menswear shop in Birmingham and measured for my first black suit and trilby. It was all very exciting. I frequently totted up the number of days until I would travel to Perth.

In my last days at St Philip's, Fathers Geoffrey and Michael Day encouraged me in my aspirations. Together with a handful of other priest aspirants, Father Michael took us one day to Cardinal Newman's room within the Oratory House itself, a rare honour for pupils who were not members of Years 12 or 13. There he showed us the original manuscript of Edward Elgar's *Dream of Gerontius.* In the summer term of 1951, I took my General Certificate of Education (GCE). Our year were the very first to take the GCE which was introduced into secondary schools that year, replacing the School Certificate.

Two days before leaving home, John and his fiancée Ann Flanagan took me to the theatre for the first and last time, since at that time it was forbidden for clerics to go to the theatre. We saw Mary Chase's *Harvey* at the Alexandra Theatre in New Street, Birmingham.

And so, aged sixteen, I was seen off at New Street station by Mum and Dad to start my new life in Perth. I changed trains in Crewe and joined Michael Creech—a fellow aspirant from the Redemptorist parish in Clapham, London.

The date was 12 July 1951.

2

Towards Priesthood during the 1950s

St Mary's, situated half-way up Kinnoull Hill in Perth, is a magnificent purpose-built monastery, completed by 1869. Funded by Father Edward Douglas, a wealthy convert to Catholicism who later entered the Redemptorist congregation, it was the first Catholic monastery to be built in Scotland since the sixteenth-century Reformation. It housed the noviciate from 1896 until 1971.

Generations of Novices were entrusted to a succession of Novice Masters, perhaps the most notable of whom was Father Joseph Ord (d. 1951). But also worthy of mention was Father Gerard Costello (d. 2005).

It was Father Costello who met Michael Creech and me off the train at Perth. We then joined ten other aspirants who, like ourselves, were proudly sporting new black suits and elegant trilby hats. We were to be joined later by a secular priest, Father Swarbrick, who was minded to continue his priesthood as a Redemptorist.

The structure of this first stage of the journey towards the priesthood had remained the same for a very long time. After a four-week period of postulancy, which included a fifteen-day silent retreat, the aspirant received the Redemptorist habit. Then began a twelve-month period of noviciate leading, after another fifteen-day silent retreat, to the taking of temporary vows. The two fifteen-day retreats were adapted from the single Jesuit thirty-day retreat, undertaken by Jesuit novices. The postulancy period overlapped with the last four weeks of noviciate of the preceding year. This enabled the postulants to be smoothly introduced to community life by the novices. Each postulant was assigned a "guardian angel".

Life in the noviciate

The daily regime was quite demanding, involving the recitation in choir of the full Liturgy of the Hours, otherwise known as the Divine Office or Breviary; three half-hour periods of meditation, again adapted from the Jesuit practice of a daily whole hour of silent prayer; two periods of manual labour; and three daily further spiritual exercises (the Rosary, Stations of the Cross and a Visit to the Blessed Sacrament). Each week there were at least three spiritual conferences.

There was also a cycle of ascetical practices, culled from the earliest days of monasticism and later observance. The Discipline, introduced by St Peter Damian in the eleventh century, was taken on Wednesdays and Fridays. A cilice was worn until after Mass on Friday. This was a metallic adaptation of the hair shirt—a medieval form of asceticism. The shirt was woven from the hair of mountain goats of Cilicia (hence the name). The modern cilice was worn around the wrist. Bitter herbs, connected with the feast of the Passover (Exodus 12:8), were taken on occasions. A series of public penances was practised in the refectory, such as begging for soup from senior members of the community.

Moreover, from these same monastic sources a number of attitudes were encouraged which aimed at mentally setting the novice increasingly apart from "the world" (that is, anything and everything on the other side of the monastic wall). It was a fault against the Rule to look out of a window, or to lose custody of the eyes. There was a prohibition against studying.

Birthdays were no longer celebrated.[1] Instead name days were marked. Individual talents were not emphasized, nor self-satisfaction allowed at the successful accomplishment of a piece of work. There was a reduction in the amount of personal privacy (each cell door had a spyhole). The Father Master could examine the contents of your correspondence. Personal decision-taking was reduced in favour of blind obedience to Superiors and to the Rule: an oft-repeated motto was "Keep the Rule so that the Rule may keep you". Novices were trained progressively "to have no will of their own".[2] In the pursuit of spiritual perfection, compliance with rules and regulations were seen as essential elements. And there were a lot of them: the Rules and Constitutions of the CSSR were the longest in the Catholic Church; the Rule itself covered twenty-two pages, with 1,678 explanatory constitutions. The whole Latin volume was over 800 pages long. Personal possessions were reduced to a minimum; instead, one asked permission for everything, even water and other small items. We used objects as if they actually belonged to somebody else. In other words, following age-long monastic tradition across most Orders and Congregations, there was a gradual self-distancing from most values that are taken for granted in normal life.

My eldest brother John and his fiancée Ann were married one month after I became a novice. I was not at their wedding. My other brother Tony (now a seminarian at Hawkstone) was not there either: the question of our attendance did not even arise, since marriage was regarded as such a "secular" thing. In the Middle Ages, it was thought that it had to be "elevated" by means of a Sacrament.

During one conference on being unworldly, this mindset was vividly communicated as follows: "When you walk through Perth, realize that everybody you see is upside down. You alone have your feet solidly on the ground."

According to the specifics of the CSSR tradition, throughout his life the Redemptorist imitates Jesus. We used straw mattresses, because Jesus slept on straw. We did not go out preaching on Missions until we were thirty, because Jesus did not begin his ministry until that age. The Redemptorist community ideally had twelve Priests and seven Brothers (cf. the priest/deacon structure of Acts 6), and so on.

More importantly there were three progressive stages in this imitation of Jesus: (a) in his early years (in the noviciate); (b) in his maturing years (in the seminary); (c) in his preaching (as a Missioner). Hence on the 25th of every month there was in the noviciate a series of exercises (compiled mainly by St Alphonsus himself) which offered the opportunity to contemplate the Divine Infant. (There was a tea party as well!) The conferences throughout the year dealt especially with twelve monthly virtues (faith, hope, love of God, fraternal charity, poverty, chastity, obedience, humility, mortification, recollection, prayer and self-denial). In practice, this meant aiming at being Carthusian-like in the monastery and an Apostle outside of it: "Carthusians at home and Apostles abroad", as St Alphonsus put it.

My diary indicates that none of this caused me any problems at all. Transition from a ghetto-orientated Catholic parish to a world-denying cloister seemed like climbing up from one rung to the next of a very tall ladder, and I was very impatient to climb as high as I could! However, one problem soon returned. During the Postulants' fifteen-day retreat, Father Donald Fraser spoke to us on the existence of God. Afterwards I went to share my problems on this basic point. I recall that he was not at all comfortable but was characteristically very anxious to help me. He assured me that all my problems would disappear when I studied this point in Philosophy at Hawkstone. I have no further record of this conversation, except that on returning to my room I concluded that just as Pythagoras had proved that, in any right-angled triangle, the square on the hypotenuse was equal to the sum of the squares on the other two sides, so St Thomas Aquinas had worked out five proofs for the existence of God which arrived at the same level of certitude. God had been restored to his place in heaven: all was once again well with the world!

So back to that ladder . . . I had the good fortune for a time to be led by a very prudent and experienced novice master, Gerard Costello, who kept my enthusiasm under control. He had succeeded Joseph Ord, having been Prefect of Students at Hawkstone for a number of years. Before that he had been a chaplain in the Royal Navy during World War II. Like myself, he too had entered the noviciate aged sixteen. For many years, it was regarded as smart to apply for admission to religious life as early as legally possible, that is sixteen years of age. St Theresa of Lisieux had actually been admitted to her convent at fifteen. By 1951, there was a further point to consider (at least as far as male religious were concerned) and that was the question of National Service. In a number of countries after the war, young seminarians were called up for National Service around their eighteenth birthday, causing much disturbance to the orderly progression towards final profession and ordination. In the UK, an arrangement was made with the British government whereby a seminarian who had already received the tonsure (the first of the minor orders) would be recognized as a cleric and so receive an exemption. Hence the need to get as many seminarians as possible tonsured before the age of eighteen.

Looking back, I am now sure that I was too young to engage meaningfully on a noviciate experience. I was the youngest of our noviciate group of thirteen aspirants. Gerard Costello was also probably conscious that I was too young and was kindness itself in my regard. For example, he forbade me from joining in the community discipline ritual, despite my frequent pleas. He was replaced as novice master in November 1951 by Father Bernard Simpson. Suddenly the regime became tougher. Bernard Simpson had been in the army and for him the noviciate should be modelled on training recruits, with very long walks, increased manual labour, and above all strict obedience—even when (and especially when) orders were clearly ill advised. He tested me to the limit when, in January, he ordered me to use floor polish (that was, candle fat and petrol) as hair cream, and when, in March, he confiscated my diaries. I took this to be a test—could I accept this intrusion into my private thoughts?—and went along with it. (In fact, I now think that he was worried about anything I might be writing about *him*!)

As I write these pages, I have my diaries open. (Yes, I did get them back.) Up to the point of confiscation I used to write about half a page a day with the reflections and reactions to all that was going on. I realize now as never before what a useful tool I have in my diaries as a means of effectively making contact across the intervening years with my actual thinking during this significant period. I had had the opportunity of hands-on experience of medieval practices and attitudes, covering many centuries of religious life. Such an opportunity was coming to an end. Very much of all that I have been describing in the last few paragraphs has now passed into oblivion—largely as a consequence of the Second Vatican Council and subsequent developments in the various Orders and Congregations. But, in our own period of ongoing change in the Church, led and inspired by Pope Francis, I think that it is important not to lose sight of where we as Catholics have come from—in order to have a clearer vision of where we may be going to.

Having survived all the subsequent tests and trials, twelve (out of the original thirteen) of our group were duly allowed to make temporary profession on 15 August 1952. Profession involves taking three vows—poverty, chastity and obedience—for a period of three years. Mum, Dad and John were present. It was a day of great joy.

From noviciate to seminary

The following day, we travelled by train from Perth to Hodnet, from where we were driven the three miles to Hawkstone Hall. The approach was down the one-and-a-half-mile drive from Marchamley to the imposing and very impressive frontage.

Hawkstone Hall is a Grade 1 listed edifice with a long history reaching back to the sixteenth century. In 1492, Roland Hill was born in Burford, Oxfordshire. He became Lord Mayor of London in 1549 and was a friend of Henry VIII. He acquired Hawkstone in 1556, and over the following three centuries the Hill family developed and richly embellished the Hall into its present appearance. In 1895, the 3rd Viscount Hill went bankrupt and the Hall passed through thirty years of uncertainty until the Redemptorists bought it in 1926.

Once again, the Redemptorists were looking for an appropriate setting for their seminary as Erdington Abbey had quickly proved to be too small. In any case, Erdington was fast becoming too urbanized for contemporary taste in terms of seminary settings. The general feeling at the time was that seminarians, especially religious seminarians, should proceed through their six years of training for the priesthood in a remote and rural setting. The Jesuit seminary was in Heythrop, near Woodstock in rural Oxfordshire; the Passionists were isolated in Minsteracres in Yorkshire; the Dominicans in Hawkesyard in Staffordshire; the De Montford fathers in nearby Church Stretton; the Claretians in Highcliffe Castle, Dorset, and so on. In this context, rurally remote Hawkstone must have seemed ideal with its commanding views across to Wales, its peace and tranquillity, temperate climate and above all its isolation.

We were greeted very enthusiastically by the Rector, the legendary Father "Pod" Hawkins, and by the whole community. Among the students was my brother Tony, now beginning his fifth year. We twelve new students quickly settled in.

Student life in Hawkstone

After life in the noviciate, life as a student was notably more relaxed. The daily routine kept one occupied for most of each day, but during periods of free time there were many acres of garden to roam in—and work in!—and much scope for scores of interesting walks and cycle rides. There were facilities for football, cricket, tennis and bowls. The students had a generously-sized common room. Mind-improving activities included a literary society, a debating society, a choir (I myself was to become choirmaster for three years) and more. Each summer we would spend two weeks at a holiday house by the sea. Parents were allowed to visit for up to a week annually.

There is one detail in the history of Hawkstone Hall that I have always remembered with affection and not a little admiration. With the cessation of hostilities after World War II, the demobbed Redemptorist students in Germany had nowhere to continue their studies. So they were welcomed to Hawkstone to join their English confreres until such time as their own seminary could be rebuilt. One English student at the time, Jimmy Mythen, who was to become a lifelong friend, colleague and adviser of mine, took this opportunity of learning German. This was to stand him in good stead on a number of occasions in his later life—notably when he was able to follow a course of theology at the University of Bonn.

There is a story attached to this period of Hawkstone history. At the time, the Prefect of Studies was Gerard Costello, who had recently been released from the Royal Navy where he had served as a naval chaplain during the war. He and one of the German students were chatting after lunch one day. The student had served in a German U-boat, and as they chatted, they both became aware that at one point his submarine had been trying to sink his Father Prefect's Royal Navy vessel!

There was another forward-looking feature of Hawkstone life—there was never any colour bar, and there were a number of non-white students. I was personally involved in helping a twenty-six-year-old Indian confrere from South Africa who had just completed his noviciate in Kinnoull. This was Brother Stephen Naidoo: I was assigned to him as his "guardian angel". One of the first challenges was to make him feel comfortable walking around the countryside. This was, after all, Shropshire in 1955.

The good folk of nearby Hodnet village would peer from behind their curtains, astonished and possibly discomfited at the sight of a black youth in a clerical collar. He and I persevered. After a number of walks we determined to face Shrewsbury. I was going to the library there, and Father Prefect asked me to take Steve along too. I was conscious of the ordeal he was patiently confronting. But we pulled it off; he felt more confident thereafter.

After his ordination to the priesthood and canon law studies in Rome, he returned to South Africa. In 1973, he was consecrated the first black Archbishop of Cape Town. An outspoken opponent of apartheid, he befriended Nelson Mandela, corresponded with him and visited him in prison on Robben Island. He was briefly detained in custody himself in March 1988. He and Archbishop Desmond Tutu led a protest procession from St George's Anglican Cathedral in Cape Town to Parliament Square, where they were confronted by the police and arrested. Nelson Mandela was always grateful to him for his support and friendship. Sadly, Steve died prematurely some eight months before Mandela was released from prison in 1990.

Back to life at Hawkstone: the seating arrangements in the refectory—we always sat in order of seniority—were such that the most junior students sat opposite the most senior. This meant, among other things, that I (the most junior) was opposite Jimmy Mythen and his year. One day these seniors were discussing some abstruse point of moral theology: was such and such a sin or not? We juniors listened attentively and bemusedly, not presuming to intervene. As often, we were at length invited to say what we thought. Jokingly I asked if they had heard of Experimental Theology.

"That has *got* to be a contradiction in terms!" Deacon Mythen intoned.

Flattered by the attention from this highest echelon of student life, I went on to make the following suggestion. "Want to find out if something is a sin? Easy! Do the thing. Go to Communion. See how you feel."

From their reaction, I somehow felt that Experimental Theology would not be added to the curriculum just yet.

The traditional six-year seminary curriculum had not changed much since the Council of Trent (1545–63), which had launched the seminary as part of its response to the Protestant Reformation. Two years of Philosophy led on to four years of Theology, with Church History, Scripture and Canon Law running alongside.

Two years before I arrived in Hawkstone, however, one change was made: the course was extended from six to seven years. After a noviciate year in which study was prohibited, young students were finding it difficult immediately to get their heads around abstract philosophical concepts, especially metaphysics. Another factor was that, with postulants being admitted earlier, students were arriving at ordination to the priesthood somewhat before they had reached the required age of twenty-four.

And this is where the story of *Posting the Word* begins!

Experiencing distance learning

This extra year involved taking part in a correspondence course with Wolsey Hall, Oxford. Founded in 1894, Wolsey Hall pioneered distance learning degree courses. For half a century from the 1930s, it provided degree-level courses in conjunction with London University's External Degree programme. Among a number of famous former course participants are Harold Evans, Editor of the *Sunday Times* between 1967 and 1981, and (most notably) Nelson Mandela, who worked through his Wolsey Hall course materials from his prison on Robben Island. (I wonder if he and Steve Naidoo, as fellow Wolsey Hall students, ever compared notes and recollections!)

The actual courses that our year followed comprised Logic, together with other courses which varied according to our individual needs. I was enrolled for two A levels—English and Latin.

I found this particular mode of study quite intimidating at first. Demanding too. We had to keep to a Study Programme, with written work to be submitted to a postal tutor at regular intervals. Our essays were duly returned to us with comments and evaluation. If we encountered problems while working through our course materials, there was the Question Sheet. One question could be articulated and submitted on the front side of a Question Sheet: the tutor's reply on the reverse side would then be returned to us. (These features may well strike a chord with the 13,000 course participants of Life Light Home Study Courses.)

For me, this was the beginning of seven years of distance learning study under Wolsey Hall, leading eventually to the Bachelor of Arts External Degree from London University in 1959. Of course, I did not know it at the time, but this was to prove a valuable experience for later. It gave me a hands-on experience of what it is like to undertake a course of study by distance learning—its anxieties, uncertainties and agonies as well as its fulfilments. As a result, I have always had a belief in the validity and potential of this type of study, as well as a deep empathy for the situation of the distance learning course participant.

Studying for the priesthood in the 1950s

What was it like following a seminary course in the 1950s? The answer is—very different from today. For one thing, there was very little academic freedom. Learning was largely modelled on the tap-and-bucket process: information flowed from the lecturer to the student. The bucket was inspected at examination time to see how much had been retained. For each curriculum subject there was a course book, called a Manual. This was in Latin. If you wanted to read around a particular topic, you had to present the book of your choice to the Superior for permission and approval.

How had the Church reached this point? In general, the aim of the seminary syllabus was to direct the seminarian towards the best of contemporary human knowledge in a philosophy course. Then, a theology course aimed to show how this interfaced with revelation and tradition. This was in line with Christian history. St Augustine (354–430) took the best of the then current philosophy, Middle Platonism, and synthesized this with the gospel. St Thomas Aquinas (1224–74) similarly linked Aristotelianism to a reinterpretation of the gospel in the light of current thinking in his famous *Summa Theologica*. This new school of thinking was known as "Scholasticism".

During the nineteenth century, there was a change in this pattern. By then, human knowledge had made enormous strides in the fields of science, technology, history and so on, but, for a number of reasons, no official reinterpretation was forthcoming from the magisterium of the Church. Instead, there was an official revival of the synthesis with medieval learning made by Thomas Aquinas—"Neo-scholasticism", which seminaries were henceforth obliged to teach. In keeping with the Vatican-directed "certainty" approach to Church teaching, the delivery of this curriculum was closely monitored. For example, the various Manuals had to be approved by the General House in Rome, and only changed with its permission. This period lasted until the Second Vatican Council (1962–5).

Hence, I completed my seminary studies at the tail-end of the pre-Vatican II period. This enabled me to acquire deep and useful insights into neo-scholastic thinking, which would prove invaluable later in the construction of the Life Light modules.

Despite this strict uniformity of philosophical and theological approach, during my time at Hawkstone cracks were beginning to appear. Father Charles Murray, one of my lecturers in philosophy, expressed doubts about certain points that he was required to teach. As the decade progressed, students' questioning in the moral theology lectures in particular became increasingly acerbic. Over recent decades moral theology had looked at times as if it was merely an extension of canon law. The Code of Canon Law had appeared in 1917, a masterpiece of clear, legal thinking that was greeted with much enthusiasm. Would it not be great (it was urged) if there could be such clarity and certainty about *everything* in our moral lives—from how to run our businesses to the details of our married lives?

I recall much debate about the line to be drawn between what constituted a venial sin and a mortal sin in theft. For a time, stealing £4.99 was a venial sin, while stealing £5.00 was a mortal sin. Who was the referee here that decided this line of demarcation? What about inflation? Sometimes this legalistic way of thinking generated funny stories. Here's one.

Fresh from the Pearly Gates, a priest and another man had just been sentenced by St Peter to hell. They were discussing their sentences.

"Why are you here?" asked the priest.

"I was the commandant of Auschwitz concentration camp," his new companion confessed. "I routinely tortured my prisoners, saw off about one million Jews and Roma travellers, raped scores of women prisoners, embezzled millions of deutschmarks and abandoned my wife after the war. What did you do?"

"I fell asleep before saying Compline."

Compline is the final Hour of the Divine Office. Omitting any part of the Office by a priest (who was committed to praying the whole Office each day) was regarded at the time as a mortal sin.

Meanwhile, some of us began to question some of the Hawkstone practices; for example, the timings of the recitation of the various Hours of the Office. For decades, both in the noviciate and now at Hawkstone, we recited Vespers and Compline just after midday. "Why do we wish God 'Goodnight!' and then go for lunch?"

So . . . what about God?

In my third year, I eventually arrived at that point in the philosophy course where we examined the proofs for the existence of God—Natural Theology. This section of the philosophy course considered all that we might know about God with the unaided use of reason. As I now review my Natural Theology notes, I am aware that I took it very seriously. I was looking for that "Pythagoras level" of proof. I didn't find it! But I really gave it my best shot.

The course considered St Thomas Aquinas' five proofs in great detail. I discovered that they depended for their cogency upon metaphysics (which we had studied the previous term) and the speculations of Aristotle (384–22 BC). There is a common thread running through them all: causality. Whatever moves is moved by something else, in a cause-and-effect relationship. But, the argument goes, we cannot go back indefinitely assigning causes to effects. We cannot say that the explanation of movement may be found in an infinite chain of causes, in an eternal universe. The only alternative is to affirm an uncaused cause. The last line of the proof was "And everybody calls this Uncaused Cause God".

I had a problem with that last line. By 1955, there were many who did *not* call such a being God! The last line seemed to need an act of faith for the Uncaused Cause to be indeed affirmed as God. (The First Vatican Council made it an article of faith that the existence of God could be proved from reason.) The proofs seemed to work only if you already believed, or knew, that there is a God. I moved on from this course to the next one, somewhat disappointed but ready to make that act of faith.

I recall one further effect on me from this course: I felt that God was now much farther away from me than when I was in the noviciate.

In search of a mystical experience

It was around this time during my third year that I got engrossed in the writings of St John of the Cross (1542–91). E. Allison Peers had produced a fresh translation of *Dark Night of the Soul*, *Ascent of Mount Carmel* and *Living Flame of Love* in three handsome volumes. I spent the best part of a year absorbing these poems, creating copious and very detailed notes. As one who, as a young man, aimed high in whatever I undertook, I sought to inject the challenging demands of St John of the Cross into my life of prayer and contemplation. *Dark Night of the Soul* is demanding in the extreme. It suggests that the path to union with God involves emptying oneself of everything which appeals to the senses and to the intellect, so that God may then fill the vacuum. For example, faced with any choice, one routinely selects that which is less desirable over that which is more desirable. At our evening meal, both tea and cocoa were on offer. I preferred cocoa—and so I took tea. This constantly presented difficulties. I liked studying for my BA degree. But *should* I like it? How could I study something effectively while maintaining a spirit of detachment from what I was studying?

For my Wolsey Hall study I sometimes had to cycle to Shrewsbury Library for course books. There were two feasible routes: one via Hodnet, the other via Preston Brockhurst. The Hodnet route was the smoother road but one mile longer than the Preston Brockhurst route which passed through more pleasant scenery. I would agonize over which route to take!

As a measure of the depth to which I entered into this mystic way, my diary contains an attempt at expressing poetically some of St John of the Cross' thoughts:[3]

'Twas in the innermost cellar of my love,
far, far away from all,
that he made me drink of love divine.
O wine without compare
which made me live for him alone!
The flock of thoughts and vain desires
now bound away and leave me free.
My will is love itself.
I have no more remembrance, mind or will
for aught but God alone.
Nor do I taste, nor see, nor hear.
'Twas there I gave myself to him
indeed, reserving nothing.
There I promised to be one with him.
Stricken with love, I wandered in the grove,
from human cares at last set free—
I cared not for the vain desires of men—
and lost myself in God.
And then he gazed on me all smilingly
as when the sun breaks through a leaden sky.
He gazed and, for his gaze, he loved the more.
We loved and loved and all was joy.
The common fields of recreation
see me now no more.
If anyone ask where I am hiding—
where I now find my delight—
Tell them: while I sought my love,
I lost my way—and was found!

The Hawkstone gardens offered opportunities for prayerful solitude. My favourite path was a short stretch to the east of the Hall beyond the rose garden. There I would walk, my mind as empty as I could manage, expecting, waiting . . . waiting for the sun to break through.

Nothing ever happened!

At the time I supposed that I had got something wrong, that I had not followed St John of the Cross' instructions correctly. So I read widely for help: Thomas Merton, the American mystic; Etienne Gilson, the French philosopher; Augustine Baker, author of *Holy Wisdom*; Leonard Boase, a Jesuit spiritual writer; St Bernard of Clairvaux, founder of the Cistercian Order; Dom Cuthbert Butler and others. It was from Butler's *Western Mysticism*, published in 1922 when he was a monk at Downside, that I drew most help. His book is a most informative description of the whole field of mystical prayer and experience throughout Europe. In his introduction, he disarmingly states that he never in fact became aware of anything which could be described as a mystical experience. This made me feel much better!

Mind-expanding trips

There were many advantages in belonging to an international religious order. One of these was student exchanges with neighbouring provinces during the summer holidays. Two or three foreign students would holiday at Hawkstone, while the same number would travel to Europe—usually, France, Belgium or Germany. Because, as part of my BA course, I was studying French by distance learning, I was sent to the Belgian province's seminary at Beauplateau in the Ardennes one year, and to Brittany and Paris in 1957 to improve my spoken French.

As my companion I was assigned Tony Hodgetts, a fellow parishioner from Erdington. The six-week-long trip went more or less smoothly. However, at one stage of our tour, a prankster gave Tony and myself an inaccurate address for the small Redemptorist house in Paris—a number in the *Rue* de Montparnasse, instead of the same number in the *Boulevard* de Montparnasse. Dressed in full Redemptorist habit, complete with dangling rosary, we presented ourselves at the first address and were sweetly, politely and helpfully directed to the second. We recounted our story at supper in the monastery. Much uncontrollable laughter: we had visited a brothel!

It was while sharing in the life of the French confreres in 1957, both while camping in Brittany and later at their seminary house in Dreux, Eure-et-Loir, that I first became aware that change in the Church was in the air. The "cracks" mentioned above had appeared in the European provinces much earlier than at Hawkstone. They had already moved on further into fresh thinking in the fields of theology and to fresh practices in the liturgy.

I met Père Danet, the Morals lecturer. He had recently translated into French the ground-breaking *Das Gesetz Christi* of the Redemptorist Father Bernard Häring (1912–98).[4] In place of the heavily legalistic emphasis in morals (mentioned above), Bernard Häring proposed a return to the Christian sources. We should find our inspiration to lead moral lives from Jesus himself, as a response to his call to us to follow him. Père Danet celebrated the Eucharist for us students on a number of occasions during the holiday. His homilies shared this new approach. They were a breath of fresh air.

Part of the students' holiday was a silent retreat towards the end of it. This was given that year by the celebrated Redemptorist Père F-X Durrwell (1912–2005), famous for the contribution he made in *The Resurrection*[5] to our understanding of the resurrection of Jesus within the story of our redemption. In his retreat conferences, he invited us to make more of our imitation of Jesus. He distinguished the *external* imitation mentioned earlier (sleeping on straw and so on) from a more *internal* imitation. We were to "put on the Lord Jesus Christ" (Romans 13:14) and identify and interiorize his mindset and values in terms of daily living in the world.

My final seminary year was spent in Echternach in the Grand Duchy of Luxembourg, which belonged to the Redemptorist Strasbourg province, of which Père Durrwell was the Superior. I once had occasion during that year to discuss *The Resurrection* with him. In the course of our conversation, he shared with me the experience of actually writing it, during the Second World War. The Nazis had commandeered the seminary, occupying all but one of the community's corridors. Life was hard. Distractions were many. He resolved that he would aim to write at least one-and-a-half lines of his book every day. So *that* is how some great works painfully reach the light of day!

I was impressed also by the attitudes of the student body to the Hours of the Divine Office. In Hawkstone, the lecturer in Dogmatic Theology had a reputation for reading the first part of the following day's Office—Matins and Lauds—at the stroke of midday (a practice called "anticipation"). The rest of the day's Office—Prime, Terce, Sext, None, Vespers and Compline—he would recite the following day before his first morning lecture. Somewhat similar practices were widespread: they were derogatively labelled as "getting your Office in". By contrast, in Dreux the students would make the various Hours more meaningful. Compline was recited last thing at night and made into a genuine Night Prayer. The other Hours were spread over the course of the day, as near as practicable to the time originally envisaged: Matins and Lauds first thing in the morning, followed by Prime and Terce after breakfast; Sext before lunch; None afterwards; Vespers at some time in the evening. (The names derive from the hours named in the Gospels: Prime = first hours (06.00); Terce = third hour (09.00), Sext = sixth hour (12.00) and None = ninth hour (15.00).)

Back in Hawkstone I began to take a very deep interest in the Office. My diaries have pages and pages of the fruits of my research and analysis into each Hour. I was due to be ordained sub-deacon the following Easter (1958), from which point one took on the obligation of the daily recitation of the full Office. I was determined to be fully prepared.[6] We were two years from the announcement by Pope John XXIII of the Second Vatican Council. However, there were already signs that a breakthrough was on the cards which would involve many changes to our way of life. The early years of many UK seminarians had been spent in an ambiance of certainty. Now, these were facing a period of increasing uncertainty in theology and Church structures.

Despite this I would at this point emphasize, contrary to what may be thought, that we students were a very happy community of young men! We led very isolated lives: I remember one year greeting my mother as she arrived for the permitted annual holiday and reflecting that I had not encountered any other female since she left a year earlier. Yet life at Hawkstone during the 1950s was generally a happy period for most of us, but there were to be many challenges during the 1960s.

I was ordained a priest along with Michael Creech in St Mary's, Clapham, on 19 October 1958. A week later I was celebrant at my first "High" Mass back at Erdington Abbey. Tony was deacon and Uncle Chris was subdeacon. The bellringers did us proud beforehand and afterwards.

There was a banquet in the Abbey Hall with about fifty guests—including Father Geoffrey Walmsley from the Oratory—and of course all the family.

It was a very happy day!

3

Living Through the Second Vatican Council

On 25 January 1959, Pope St John XXIII made a surprise announcement. There was to be another ecumenical Council, and it would be held at the Vatican. His predecessor Pius XII had wanted to call a short Council in 1948, but he was not sufficiently supported by senior members of the Curia. (The Curia dates from Sixtus V (1585–90). With the concerns of the Council of Trent in mind, he organized an efficient and highly centralized system of justice and administration, comprising Congregations, Tribunals and Offices. By the twentieth century, it had grown to become very powerful.) Pope John XXIII made his announcement directly to the Church at large. The Curia officials had no choice but to cooperate. This event was to change the lives of millions of Catholics in a number of ways. In my own case, it was to lead to the development of Life Light, as we shall see.

For the moment, I want to try to communicate something of the excitement and general enthusiasm in many of us who had a more particular interest in what was going on at the Council. Hopefully this will enable a clearer appreciation of Life Light and what it set out to do.

Training to teach

I returned from Echternach in June 1959 and took my BA examination. Two days later I had to do my seminary finals. By the time of the summer holidays, I felt thoroughly examined!

I was then sent to Liverpool University to do a Post-Graduate Certificate in Education (PGCE) course prior to taking up a teaching post in our Junior Seminary, known as the "Juvenate", at Erdington Abbey. The course consisted of 50 per cent lectures in educational theory in the University and 50 per cent teaching practice in and around the city. For teaching practice, I was sent to two Catholic schools: St Edward's, Sandfield Park, followed by St John Almond's secondary school in Garston.

In those days, PGCEs were much more leisurely than they were later to become. I was able to do a lot of "firsts" as a new priest—sermons, pastoral work around Liverpool, counselling, confessions and so on. I warmed to Liverpudlians and enjoyed their stories, like the one about the philosophy professor who was travelling by train from London to Liverpool. In actual fact, his destination was close to the (now closed) station at Edge Hill—the last on the line before Liverpool's principal station, Lime Street. As luck would have it, his train made an unscheduled stop at Edge Hill station and so (as you could in those days) he opened the carriage door and alighted.

"Hey! You!" shouted a railway member of staff. "This train hasn't stopped here!"

"That's quite all right," replied the philosopher. "I'm not getting off!"

This story reminds me that during those early days of hearing confessions there was sometimes "and I got off at Edge Hill". Taking this to be fare dodging I used to give brief exhortations to higher standards of honesty and practical advice on how British Rail could be compensated. I later discovered that in the Liverpool area the reference was to interrupted lovemaking!

A happy community—snapshots

I completed my PGCE in July 1960. Then it was back to my native Erdington in September to start teaching full-time in the Juvenate. (Mum was delighted to have her son back after ten years absence.) For my PGCE, I had taken options in English, French and History Method.

Once arrived in the Juvenate, I was told to teach Music, Geography and—yes!—French. (This used to happen quite often in religious life.)

There were six of us—all priests—teaching between forty and fifty Juvenists, aged between eleven and eighteen. New premises had just been built, attached to the Abbey itself, and there was a general feeling of optimism among the teaching staff.

While I was in Echternach, some office-holder changes had been made, one of which appointed my Uncle Chris to the position of Rector and Parish Priest of Erdington Abbey—in other words *my* superior! This did not work out well. When disgruntled confreres needed to air a grievance, they would sometimes approach me and ask me to raise the matter with Uncle Chris. At the same time, in a busy parish like Erdington, there was always a whole host of large and small jobs which needed to be done. If Chris did not fancy approaching a senior member of the community, he would all too often take the softer option and simply ask me to oblige. So on arrival to teach in the Juvenate, I was required to assume the role of parish choirmaster and lots more. Hence my first year was rather well occupied.

For the greater part of the 1960s, we were a community of around twenty: fourteen priests and six brothers. Most of us were aged under forty and very active in our various community assignments. There was a warm, at times jolly, atmosphere.

Sometimes this jollity was misunderstood, as when, just after Christmas in 1960, Father John Howard died very suddenly at a great old age. Because of the sudden nature of his death—he had a fall the day before—the police had to make enquiries. On the day Father Howard died two police constables arrived while the community were at lunch. They were looking for the Rector to take a statement and to examine Father Howard's room.

While they were doing this, the woman constable was quizzing Uncle Chris about any enemies that the deceased might have had. Chris was puzzled. He assured her that Father Howard didn't have any enemies. And she said, "Well, it doesn't sound very much like it!" She pointed in the direction of the refectory. "I mean, just listen to that party going on down there! He only died this morning! Are they rejoicing over the death of someone they didn't like too much?"

So Chris was at pains to explain the Redemptorist attitude to the death of a confrere—that we could celebrate a man's life with joy; it wasn't a question of rejoicing over an enemy but rejoicing over a life well lived. Chris avoided arrest and the police officers went off satisfied but perhaps still a little curious.

Uncle Chris was eventually appointed to Liverpool, where he died in 1966.

Our next Superior incorporated a Golden Retriever into our Abbey community. (The Redemptorist Rule, in Constitution 507, forbade pets.) He announced his name as "Sam". Other confreres had other names—"Marmaduke", "Piddles" (to rhyme with "Tiddles" the Abbey cat), and others. Father Francis Brazier began calling the middle corridor "the Lake District"—a reflection of the need for care when using this puddle-prone passage. With reference to our very senior confreres, our Maths teacher was heard to declare: "Still, if you don't quite make it to the toilet, it's consoling to know that the Rector will mop up your mess for you!"

Living through the Council

The small Juvenate staff continued to deliver a grammar school type of curriculum, and some of us taught multiple subjects. The headmaster was Jimmy Mythen, who had completed his own PGCE the year before me and who taught Latin and Greek. History was very ably taught by Henry Parker (my own Church History lecturer at Hawkstone). In charge of Mathematics was Beverley Ahearn, while Bernard Crowe taught RE and English.

Alongside our teaching, Vatican II was taking place in St Peter's in Rome between 1962 and 1965. Before class, we would rush to grab *The Times* for its daily report on the proceedings in the Council the day before. Most days there was an accurate and reliable account of the Council Fathers' deliberations—*The Times* managed to get it right the following morning whereas other papers failed to do so by the following weekend! During those three years there was never any lack of things to talk about in the community. Deep and detailed changes to our lives as Catholics were coming through to us—at times on a daily basis:

- For centuries the Mass had been said in Latin—now it was going to be celebrated in English.
- "The faith" used to mean sets of propositions—now it meant a way of life as well.
- "The Church" had long been taken as a reference to the clergy for the most part—now it was going to be *all* of us—the People of God.
- The laity used to be at the bottom of the pile—now Pope and peasant were both equal by virtue of baptism.
- Ministry used to mean dominative power—now it meant service.

. . . And very much more.

The Council was not all plain sailing by any means. Less than two months in from the start, following an intervention by Cardinal Suenens of Brussels, every one of the preparatory commissions' schemata for the various council documents was rejected and sent back for complete revision. It all made for exciting reading!

We were thus able in some measure, over the three-year period of Vatican II, to live the experience on a daily basis. In this sense it was a learning curve—steep at times (for example, during the long discussions of the *Constitution on Revelation*). It took me a long time to get my head round the new way of looking at the mechanics of revelation in the Bible. At Hawkstone, we had come close to seeing biblical texts as having been almost dictated by God himself to a series of human authors. By contrast, at the Council there was talk of revelation being seen as "interpreted activity"—with us humans doing the interpreting. Experiencing the Council was thus like travelling along a road, from a familiar departure point towards a destination where there would be a new way of looking at ourselves, the Church and the world. Not all of us travelled this road at the same speed. Some of the more senior members of the community ambled along at a gentler pace.

However, when it eventually came to "selling" these new ideas to the Abbey parishioners, we achieved a remarkable consensus of opinion as to how to go about this. We wanted, as far as possible, to show a unity of approach from the pulpit. An example of this presented itself when the Mass started to be celebrated in English after the conclusion of the

Council. To promote acceptance by our good and faithful parishioners, we decided after a series of community meetings to present a united front. On the first day of the new English Mass, we would all show confidence and enthusiasm for it. We would make it *seem* as if we had been celebrating Mass this way for years.

This policy worked—in the main. However, one of our veteran missioners displayed overconfidence at one point. At Communion, the priest holds up the host and used to say "Ecce Agnus Dei . . . " ("Behold the Lamb of God . . . "). Our enthusiastic confrere held up the host and declared: "Behold the handmaid of the Lord!", to which the confused congregation replied: "Be it done unto me according to thy word!", words taken from the Angelus prayer rather than from the Mass. It all made us realize that we had a lot of catechizing to do!

Another example of our enthusiasm for the Council occurred in January 1966. We received the text of the Council *Decree on Religious Life*, which had been passed the previous month. Among the many changes envisaged in this document, paragraph 2(d) wanted religious to have an "awareness of contemporary human conditions". I recall Jimmy Mythen coming to my room the same day. Could we perhaps launch a Current Affairs course in Year 12? Eventually this morphed into a course leading to the Oxford Local Examinations Economics O level exam, which I ran for a number of years. I think that this short course benefited many boys—we had a lot of passes. It was to help me as well at a later stage when dealing with the financial details of setting up Life Light.

Vatican II did not have much to say about Junior Seminaries; it was all contained in a single paragraph, "Decree on Priestly Formation 3". This was because opinion was sharply divided among the Council Fathers as to whether they should exist at all. We Juvenate teachers also displayed a growing feeling that there was something intrinsically wrong about taking boys before puberty and setting them on a road which leads to a life of celibacy. So, with the approval of my colleagues, I started work on future options for the Juvenate. During the summer vacation of 1965, I visited the French Juvenate in Mouscron (Belgium) to compare notes and hopefully get some fresh ideas. Too late! The French Juvenate had just closed! But I did pick up a lot of visual aids to help with my French classes.

Eventually I drew up a plan to transform our 11–18 school into a Sixth Form College. Later, in the light of a Vatican document, *The Renewal of Religious Formation* (6 January 1969), I updated the Sixth Form College proposal to make it a two-year Postulancy, as described in the document. The proposal was adopted in October 1969.

It was not just our Erdington community that was initially enthusiastic about Vatican II. The General Superior in Rome decided to reform the Redemptorists while Vatican II was still in session. It was actually during the Council itself that arrangements were being made to hold a General Chapter to rewrite our long Rule. By 1969, this work was complete. There were many changes to our way of life. For example, we began voting for our Superiors.

Travelling the road

Paul VI closed the Second Vatican Council on 8 December 1965, and the bishops dispersed homewards. The following month our Archbishop (George Patrick Dwyer) was due to ordain two confreres priests in the Abbey Church. His Grace insisted that we install a new altar to enable him to celebrate Mass facing the people, as his fellow bishops at the Council would now be doing. Our parishioners were not at all ready for this culture shock. Afterwards they were clearly divided on the issue.

Nowadays most eucharistic services are performed with the priest facing the congregation. But at that point, one month after the close of the Council, many people were taken by surprise. Over the intervening years I have given much thought to this episode. To return to the concept of "travelling a road", I think that we in the community had no problem with the Archbishop celebrating Mass with his face to the people. We had been living the day-to-day deliberations in the Vatican—just as his Grace had. We had travelled a road during the course of which our mindsets had *gradually* been changed. There is a lot of evidence that the bishops too underwent a huge and at times steep learning curve during the course of the three-year Council. By the end of this experience, they were able to vote with impressive majorities for the various documents. Archbishop George Patrick seemed to realize all too little that most of his congregation on this occasion had *not* been travelling that same road since 1962. There had initially been a widespread idea that, because the Council was being labelled an "ecumenical" affair, it was principally about Rome and Canterbury reuniting. In 1966, few people in the pew could tell you much about what had been going on in Rome. So, when faced with a sudden and dramatic change like the bishop facing the congregation, the faithful divided into enthusiasts and sceptics. Some parishioners welcomed the novelty, others pined for the good old days of the Benedictines. All would have welcomed some warning!

On this occasion, the Archbishop had given the impression that he was relying too much on the pre-Vatican II idea of the laity being people who "paid, prayed and obeyed" and did not require explanations. But times had changed.

A comprehensive new drive to educate our Catholic laity was needed. They needed vehicles to enable them to travel the road. Books and publications quickly began to appear which explained Vatican II in straightforward terms. The Grail Community produced simplified versions of the main Council documents. There would have to be a number of new initiatives, not all of them just at parish level. Priests, headteachers and teachers of RE would need to be updated. Pastoral centres sprang up in many dioceses to meet this urgent need. There was even a National Centre in Corpus Christi College in Bayswater, London, set up with the help of the Lumen Vitae International Catechetical Centre in Brussels. What could a mere teacher of French in a Junior Seminary do to help?

The Catholic publishing firm Sands & Co approached the community in 1966 for someone to translate *Christianisme et Civilisations* by Jean de Fabrègues, a 500-page volume of background reading to the Council by a leading historian of ideas. The request landed on my desk as French teacher, and I started work on it straight away. The book identifies the relationship in history between Christianity and each of the major civilizations (Hindu, Western European and Islam). It suggests that, while there is no such thing as a Christian civilization, Christian values have much to say to each of the world's civilizations. Much of the text cast light on several Vatican II documents, even though many of the ideas predated the Council.

Chasing up Fabrègues' thousand-odd footnotes got me into the magnificent Reading Room of the old British Museum. In many other ways, this task was a rewarding experience. My Reading Room pass helped greatly in the writing of the early Life Light modules.

But what about God?

During the hectic days of the early 1960s, I immersed myself in teaching, parish work and trying to make Vatican II ideas my own. My God problem hid in the recesses of my brain. Then on 8 April 1966 *Time* magazine famously announced on its front cover that "God is Dead". All my old fears and phobias returned. It was like being torpedoed yet again. Changing the simile, what if all my spiritual skyscraper constructing had no basement?

A little background to the alleged death of God. Friedrich Nietzsche (1844–1900) used the phrase "God is dead" in *Thus Spoke Zarathustra* (1885) as an assertion that the Enlightenment of the eighteenth century had rendered God unnecessary. A serious and sincere Christian response was made by Dietrich Bonhoeffer (1906–45), notably in his *Letters and Papers from Prison* (1951). The idea was taken up in the 1960s by some theologians in the United States who became known as propagating a "Death of God" theology. It was to these that *Time* magazine referred. The essential message of Christianity, they maintained, should be communicated to our secular neighbours without any reference to God, because either many modern people did not believe in God anymore (thus Gabriel Vahanian), or else the concept of God had ceased to have any of its original meaning (according to Paul van Buren), or else because God died on Calvary (Thomas Altizer), or because this was the only honest attitude to take (William Hamilton).

In November 1966, the Fathers of the Birmingham Oratory asked me to take part in a debate on this Death-of-God theology. My opponent was to be Neil Middleton, editor of *Slant* magazine, which advocated adopting Marxist models for reforming the Catholic Church.

I did a lot of preparation for this debate. I was acutely conscious that I would be back at my old St Philip's School and that I would be debating from inside a clerical collar. In the event, the debate turned out to be a most gentlemanly affair! We agreed to disagree, where appropriate; in fact, we both agreed at the end that, no matter what we thought about the Death-of-God theology, the Catholic Church should take it seriously. We should not look the other way and quietly hope that the whole thing would go away.

Looking back, I now think that this event was therapeutic in the circumstances of my chronic unsureness about the existence of God. However, I do recall a painful moment during the last fifteen minutes of the session. I suddenly asked myself: "Am I on the right side of this debate?"

Headteacher

During the autumn term of 1969 the Redemptorists held elections. We now voted for who should be our Superiors and who should occupy certain other offices. In this way, I became headteacher of the Juvenate. My task was to transform an 11–18 grammar school into a pre-noviciate postulancy (as mentioned above). This meant that 11+ entry ceased and that school numbers inevitably were reduced.

It was also the opportunity to make some changes inspired by the experience of having lived through Vatican II. The daily life of the boys now became centred around a midday celebration of the Eucharist. I tried to simplify and make more meaningful some of their spiritual exercises. For example, one of these was the daily fifteen-minute visit to the Blessed Sacrament. Traditionally use had been made of a famous and well-loved booklet, composed by St Alphonsus, comprising thirty-one brief readings for each day of the month. It seemed to me that long sections of this eighteenth-century text meant little to Juvenists. So I drew up thirty-one Gospel passages, taken from the actual quotations of what Jesus said, and arranged them under various relevant headings like "True Greatness", "The Golden Rule", "True Wealth", and so on. My idea was that, instead of imagining what Christ *might* be saying to them during their visit, the boys could experience what he *had actually* said. All this was incorporated into a new version of the *Juvenists' Prayer Book*.

Actually, I had tried to use this idea before. This was the age of Chairman Mao Zedong (1893–1976), of the Chinese Cultural Revolution (1966) and of the Little Red Book containing "The Thoughts of Chairman Mao". Our Year 9 boys obeyed their instinct for mandatory obnoxiousness by, among other things, provocatively waving their copies of the Little Red Book on all sorts of occasions. My reaction was to engage with them on a project to create another little red book entitled "The Thoughts of Chairman Jesus". We would take the Sayings of Jesus from the four Gospels—all the bits inside inverted commas—and reassemble them under various headings. Their enthusiasm for my project was predictably short-lived. (Chairman Mao bit the dust as well!) But I developed my idea into what I thought was a publishable approach to prayer. The manuscript was sent to a number of Catholic publishers.

However, in the first place the manuscript had to go through censorship. At the time, whenever a confrere wanted to publish any work, two priests, whose identities were not to be made known to the author, were appointed by the Father Provincial to examine the work for theological errors. In the case of the *Thoughts of Jesus*, the first censor completed his work within a week and made one comment. The second censor sat on my manuscript for two months and had to be prodded into action by the Provincial. He had no comment to make.

One of the publishers to whom I sent my manuscript was Sheed and Ward (since I had recently become known to them through Neil Middleton). Rosemary Sheed wrote me a most encouraging letter. However, by that time someone at the Catholic Truth Society had had a similar idea and very quickly brought out a little yellow book entitled *The Thoughts of Jesus Christ*. No other publisher was thereafter interested in working on another book with a similar title. I did not make a fuss about the workings of censorship. However, I did begin to ask myself whether there might be a more efficient way of communicating one's ideas.

As headteacher I became a member of the "Formation Commission", an advisory body which had to make recommendations as to the future pattern of training for the priesthood and religious life. I drew up an ambitious report involving the removal of the Hawkstone students to London, and the setting-up of a Pastoral Centre at Hawkstone. (This was not well received at the time!)

Within a year of my appointment as headteacher, the newly formed Provincial Council decreed the full eventual closure of the Juvenate. This decision meant that there would be no Sixth Form College, or new postulancy; it would all be shut down. This presented an altogether new task: to wind down the operation of the school, and to find appropriate ongoing educational provision for each one of the Juvenists affected by this closure. This was fully accomplished by 24 June 1971 when the Juvenate finally closed. The education of not a single boy was disrupted.

Before the closure, Vicar General Father George Bérubé visited us from Rome. We teachers were to be dispersed around Europe (Dundalk in Ireland, Bonn in Germany and Lumen Vitae in Brussels) for refresher courses. I was to go to Lumen Vitae.

4

From Lumen Vitae to Life Light

Lumen Vitae

The International Centre for Catechetics, Lumen Vitae, was founded by Georges Delcuve SJ in 1954 and set up in rue Washington in Brussels. (In 2016, it moved to the University of Namur.) The principal aim of the Institute was to discern new ways of communicating the Christian way of life with the help of modern science, especially psychology.

There were two Redemptorist communities in Brussels—one for each of the two Belgian languages, French and Flemish. Since all the lectures at Lumen Vitae were in French, I chose to join the French-speaking house of St Joseph on rue Belliard. It was a home from home! I had already spent a couple of months in the Belgian province in 1956 at the seminary in Beauplateau, and so knew some of the Brussels community.

At the Institute there was an impressive opening Mass at the start of term. There were 183 students—thirty different nationalities with only the Faith and French in common. Most of the newcomers like me were properly dressed for the occasion with clerical collars or, where appropriate, veils. As the first weeks passed, the veils and the collars became rarer sights and we settled down to a slightly more secularized attire. We quickly transformed ourselves into a single group of enthusiastic seekers after post-Vatican II wisdom. Through the medium of French, we could share insights from the world over, despite our varying degrees of proficiency in the language. German–French was highly accurate. Spanish and Italian–French just flowed uncontrollably. I'm told that American–French presented the most problems!

For the students from the UK, it was an exciting time to be in Brussels. Two days after the start of term, the Westminster Parliament voted by a majority of 112 to join the European Common Market. As a result, you could not walk down any corridor without someone or other wrapping his, or usually her, arms around you by way of welcome! The Common Market headquarters in Berlaymont circularized all colleges in the city looking for native Anglophones. The idea was to hold a series of social evenings at which only English would be spoken—this was to help the Berlaymont civil servants quickly to become proficient in English before an army of UK workers crossed the Channel. These sessions consisted very pleasantly of fondue meals, either of cheese or meat, washed down with generous supplies of red and white plonk. I am not sure how much English was acquired, but it was a great introduction to the fondue!

The Licenciate course

I enrolled in 1971 for a two-year course leading to the *Licence en Catéchèse et Pastorale* awarded by the Catholic University of Louvain. I specialized in adult religious education in the first year and the theology of religious life in the second. The subject of my thesis was "God in Adult Catechetics: How to speak about God to the modern adult."

Why these particular options?

I had just lived through five years of much talk and reflection on how to renew our Redemptorist lives, and I sought firmer foundations for this process. Redemptorists were not schoolteachers; the aim of the founder St Alphonsus was to reach adults—specifically the most abandoned at any given time—and to preach the gospel in a manner appropriate for adults. In the years following the conclusion of the Council in 1965, there was a growing interest, especially throughout Europe, in adult religious education.

It was felt that religious education had in the past been focused too much on the school. Children had been progressively taught the truths of the Christian/Catholic faith up to school-leaving age, with scarce resources for any follow-up during the rest of one's life. It was widely feared that most Catholics retained this child's stage of faith awareness throughout life, generating and maintaining a less than ideal Catholic ethos. However, by the 1970s attitudes were changing. Christianity was increasingly being appreciated as, in the first place, an adult faith. Nowhere in the Gospel texts is Jesus seen as directly preaching to children. (Jesus was not being singular here. It was not the Jewish way of doing things in those days. Rabbis instructed fathers and the fathers instructed their family.) Christian faith, it was felt, interfaces with grown-up areas of concern like marriage, interpersonal relations, justice and all the areas of Catholic Social Teaching.

The 1974 Synod of Bishops in Rome saw adult RE as an absolute priority in the Church. St John-Paul II declared it "the principal form of catechesis". In the UK, the participants in the National Pastoral Congress in Liverpool (1980) were to stress its importance in every one of its sector reports. The Bishops of England and Wales, responding in *The Easter People*, were to agree with the Congress and declare their willingness to allocate "the personnel and resources that may be proved necessary".

It seemed to me that the "Redemptorist moment" had arrived. The Parish Mission, for which the Redemptorists were justly famous as one of the main providers, could be reinvented to meet the current need for post-Vatican II adult catechesis. I embarked on my course with enthusiasm.

Renewing religious life

The course on religious life was delivered mainly by Father J. M. R. Tillard OP. It contained many challenges and fresh insights. From the time of my noviciate in Perth, I had been immersed in an interpretation of religious life which originated in the distant past history of monasticism. This prioritized the vows of poverty, chastity and obedience as being the essence of religious life, aimed at promoting the perfection of its individual members, and set its face against change.

Tillard painstakingly took us through the relevant sections of Vatican II and the vast literature that had recently appeared. We learnt that our practice of poverty could not be traced back to Jesus, but rather to the Poverty Movement of St Francis of Assisi (1182–1226); that many celibatic practices had entered monasticism from sources *outside* the Judaeo-Christian tradition; and that being obedient to superiors (as a means of spiritual growth) was foreign to Jesus' thinking—he himself showed obedience only to God his Father.

On one occasion, Tillard solemnly read out a passage:

> Following the proposition of the *founder*, the members dedicated themselves to the contemplation of God's mysteries in a life of an asceticism which aimed at promoting the spirit of prayer and perfect self-control. Admission was by stages: a three-year trial of perseverance and detection of self-interest was followed by a five-year instruction under a Master who had to be shown strict obedience. All wore a distinctive habit. They accused themselves of faults committed against the common rule, which was very strict. There were periods of silence. Silence was regarded as a necessary preliminary for meeting one's fellow-men. Meals were taken in silence, while a book was publicly read.

Then he asked us: "Who do you think the "founder" was in line 1?"

We were all sisters and priests in the auditorium. We were all well positioned to have a good and credible guess. We suggested St Basil, St Dominic (Tillard was a Dominican), St Ignatius Loyola (Lumen Vitae was a Jesuit institute), etc.

The answer astounded us. It was Pythagoras—of "square of the hypotenuse" fame—and he was writing his "Rule" some six centuries before Jesus!

Was there *anything* in our way of life that was inspired by Jesus? Well, yes, there was. And Tillard gave us a brilliant and very stimulating course which put religious life on a new footing. It was more theological, healthier and more relevant to our times. His course was supplemented by a short period of time spent with the interdenominational Taizé community in France which I found very inspiring. One of the earliest Life Light modules was the *Theology of Religious Life*, and it owed very much to Tillard.

Towards a married clergy?

Discussions among our international group were frequent, always well informed and stimulating. During my two-year course, 1971–3, there was plenty to talk about. One of the issues was liberation theology and its application in communities. One of the visiting lecturers to Lumen Vitae was Gustavo Gutiérrez, founder of Liberation Theology, which sought to energize the Church towards coming to the rescue of the poor, especially in Latin America. We also discussed new movements in the Church (especially the Charismatic Movement and Marriage Encounter), and much more.

The first focal point of discussion arose with the meeting of the 1971 Roman Synod on celibacy. There were no public lectures on this issue: but there was much informal sharing of ideas and literature, such as *The origins of celibacy in the Church* by local authority R. Gryson,[1] which detailed the history of clerical celibacy, and included the information that one motivation for the imposition of clerical celibacy in 1139 was an attempt to stop clergy leaving church property to their offspring. Discussions were wide-ranging and at times tentatively called into question the celibatic state of Jesus himself. (He was a Rabbi, and in the first century all Rabbis had to be married. This point will be discussed further in Chapter 13). There was an expectation among us that the Synod would sanction a change. During the Vatican Council itself the bishops were split fifty-fifty on the issue—although the point was never put to a vote. In the event, the 1971 Roman Synod voted to maintain mandatory clerical celibacy.

Our local bishop was the world-famous Cardinal Suenens. He quite often called in to Lumen Vitae and was well known for his frank and open discussions with us. One such visit was shortly after he returned from the Synod. He was disappointed at the outcome and did not hide his feelings—especially on the question of the reliability of the final vote.

I often reflect on how things could have worked out differently if this vote had gone the other way. At the time, laicizations of priests churchwide were running at around 4,000 per annum with 3,000 ordinations per annum to the priesthood. These figures would surely have started to turn around. More speculatively, would the sad story of clerical sexual abuse of minors have read differently? Many Vatican Curial officials have consistently insisted that the abuse is nothing to do with celibacy. For what it is worth I feel that with the introduction of women into intimate clerical circles the abuse would have been exposed much earlier. They would have sniffed out any impropriety. Their screams and shouts would have made any cover-up impossible. The legal bills which have financially crippled a number of dioceses would not have been presented. And the savings would surely have more than compensated for the extra costs of maintaining presbytery homes.

Be that as it may, our *expectation* of a change exerted an influence upon how we as students conducted ourselves towards one another. In lecture rooms, the females among us tended normally to sit at the front of the auditorium, with the males at the rear. Around the period of the Synod, this pattern gradually, and not without some hesitation, gave way to more mixed seating arrangements, based loosely on language groupings. Coffee breaks began to be more mixed, as were meals in the café. One attractive feature of life in Brussels was being able to visit nearby bars in the middle of the afternoon after lectures. (Opening hours in the UK rendered this impossible at the time!) Around the time of the Synod we blokes began increasingly to be joined by the Sisters—a trend which continued even after the Synod's negative decision.

New moves on Church Unity?

Cardinal Suenens held another session at Lumen Vitae to share his enthusiasm for the Charismatic Movement and Marriage Encounter. Towards the end of this session we started to raise all sorts of questions. I remember a Spanish priest who referred to the possibility that the Cardinal could very well be voted in by the next conclave as successor to Pope Paul VI. (This was not idle talk: he was being widely supported.) He asked the Cardinal, "What would be the first thing you would do?"

After the customary "No chance!" disclaimers, the Cardinal said that he might well call another Council. This would not be Vatican III but Jerusalem II. (This was in 1971; the current troubles in that region still lay in the future.) His idea was to call a Second *Jerusalem* Council—the first one having taken place there c. AD 48 (cf. Acts 15). It would not be held in the immediate future. It would be held in the year 2000, and an invitation would be extended to *all* Christian denominations, not just to Catholics. There would be a simple theme: "These two thousand years—how has it been for you?" Between 1971 and 2000, denominations, including our own, would reflect on our different stories, produce reports and make suggestions as to how things might have been different and how they could be different in the centuries to come. If the common ground among the various denominations increased as a result of this exercise, it would be celebrated in Jerusalem. A united fresh start could be made.

We gave him a round of applause. I have never forgotten this incident. Pope Francis could well be persuaded to take it further. He recently observed how inter-denominational dialogue typically revolves around the sacrament of Order, the validity of orders, ministry, and so on, and has had limited success. He said that it might be better for it to revolve around Baptism instead. Suenens would have agreed.

Time with the family

I kept myself quite busy during my time in Brussels. I took on a large amount of translation work for the English version of *Lumen Vitae* magazine. These were mostly articles by Tillard (lecturer in Religious Life), Marcel van Caster (lecturer in Anthropology) and others. There was some locum work in outlying Belgian parishes (including my first Sung Mass in French at Villères-la-Ville on Christmas Night 1971, and a bilingual nuptial Mass and marriage ceremony in Ohain). The celebrated Christiane Brusselmans was pioneering her innovative programme of Sacramental Preparation at St John's International School near Waterloo.[2] I willingly gave a hand and felt privileged to have participated in an important stage in the history of religious education.

My brother, John, sister-in-law Ann and family were living at the time three miles from Waterloo in the picturesque village of Ohain. John was employed by Singer and did pioneering work in the early days of computer technology. He invented a "Conversational Program Generator" which was later to be hailed by the Computer History Museum in Sacramento, California, as "the first piece of application software ever written".

They sent their sons, Anthony, Michael and Stephen, to St John's School, while their daughter Marian was finishing her education at the historic English Convent School in Bruges. Ann and John's eldest son, Paul, tragically died in a car accident not far from the family home in September 1970. He was eighteen and had passed his driving test just weeks earlier in England. Our whole family was devastated. I officiated at the Requiem Mass and led the funeral liturgy. He was laid to rest in Ohain parish cemetery.

I spent many happy and refreshing weekends at John and Ann's in Ohain during my time at Lumen Vitae. They were happy times—despite the ongoing need to come to terms with what had happened and to enable life to go on.

As for me, the experience fed in to one of the many essays I wrote in connection with my Lumen Vitae course. Abbé Buissonnier delivered an inspired course on the catechesis of those in need (*Catéchèse des inadaptés*)—including the bereaved. My essay reflected on my own experience of recent bereavements in relation to Paul (aged 18), to my Uncle Chris (aged 52) and my paternal grandmother (aged 95)—three very different bereavement experiences. I researched bereavement grief and related this to the challenges and opportunities for the supportive Christian community, with special reference to the clergy. Buissonnier recommended publication. (I never got round to it.)

The thesis on God

I had enormous problems getting the subject of my thesis on God approved. "It is too vast!" my tutor Ignace Berten OP and my fellow students counselled me. "Why not take a subsection of some canon in the 1918 Code of Canon Law, analyse it from every conceivable angle, suggest how it might be improved, and so on? You'll find that much easier."

To my mind there was more at stake than merely "getting the thesis done". Now, at long last, I had the time and opportunity to confront my doubts about the existence of God. I was giving God, as it were, a last chance; if I found nothing at the end of my research—that would be it!

In the event, I found rather more than I had bargained for. As I read deeply and more widely, I felt that I was moving in a promising direction. The starting point for my thesis was the neo-scholastic God that had been rejected in the 1960s Death-of-God episode—that is, a subsistent Being whose existence could be proved and who lives apart from his creation yet intervenes every now and again for his own often mysterious purposes. (This had been the concept of God which had caused me so many difficulties in my youth.)

It was refreshing to discover the work of the German Protestant theologian Paul Tillich (1886–1966). He suggested that, when thinking about God, we should move away from the concept of "subsisting Being" to that of "Being Itself". By God we would mean the ground of our being—of all being, including his own.

I then moved on to the radical insights of Leslie Dewart (1922–2009). He wanted to abandon the concept of Being altogether—this as part of his "de-hellenization of Christianity" programme. For Dewart, the gospel had been transmitted using the concepts and assumptions of the philosophy of Ancient Greece. Many of these have now been brought into question (misogyny, static nature of the universe and so on) and, Dewart maintains, this had led to modern atheism. Dewart is content to experience the *presence* of God and abandon metaphysics altogether. This also was the later insight of the Process philosophers and theologians, such as Alfred Whitehead (1861–1947), Charles Hartshorne (1897–2000) and others. Process theology experiences God as working from the inside of his creatures. This idea is often called Panentheism, that is, God is *in* everything—as distinct from Pantheism (God *is* everything).

Then I considered the contributions made by the existentialist theologians. Rudolph Bultmann (1884–1976) advocated a demythologization of the New Testament, with a view to an eventual communication of the original kerygma of especially Paul and John using modern concepts and terminology. His approach to God proceeded via the God of Jesus and the approach of the Hebrew scriptures. The God of Bultmann is the answer to humanity's quest for authentic living.

I then turned to the theologians of hope—especially Jürgen Moltmann (1929–), Wolfhart Pannenberg (1928–2014) and Johann Baptist Metz (1928–2019). These take the wavelength of time and history as a way of comprehending God's transcendence (in place of metaphysics). God is the One who is before us, pulling humankind forward into all our futures—out of the lower states of evolution into the higher. Moltmann, in his *Theology of Hope*, shows how this mindset is rooted in the Hebrew scriptures and is present in Jesus' preaching of the kingdom of God.[3] Pannenberg also maintains that "faith in God ... can only be achieved through Jesus".[4]

In the concluding sections of my thesis, I drew together some of the insights gathered from Tillich, Dewart, Bultmann, Moltmann and the other theologians considered. I had been struck in particular by the fact that each of the proposed approaches to the reality of God was seen and valued as an answer to a question. How can I relieve the pain I feel which arises from living as a merely finite being? (Tillich) How can I escape from the absurdity of life? (Bultmann and others) What is the significance of the various phenomena of process? (Whitehead)

My thesis demonstrated that the question of our time (the 1970s) was "What is the meaning of life?" Taking a leaf out of Pannenberg's book, I showed how Jesus can help us address this question and in so doing enable us to experience the presence of his Father in our daily lives. This involved me in a detailed analysis of John 1:14—"the Word was made flesh". I collected evidence that a significant component in understanding the term "Word"—λόγος / logos in Greek—is "meaningfulness". The Ancient Greek convert to Christianity reading John 1:14 would have understood that, with the coming of Jesus, "life's meaning" had taken human form in our world. It is not that Jesus ever revealed to us the actual meaning of life. What he did do was to outline a way of life that enables us to lead lives *in harmony* with the meaning of life.

An important aspect of the Christian way of life is one's attitude to the Transcendent. Jesus wants this to be modelled on a Father-child relationship. Nature, the beyond, the cosmos, is therefore friendly; it can be explored and investigated without the fear of repercussions. That "Father" lived in Jesus; he told us that he lives in us too. Jesus' use of "Abba" when addressing the Father (as in Mark 14:36) is an indication, not only of how close Jesus knew God was to himself as a human being, but also of how close he knew God was to *all* of us (cf. Romans 8:15; Galatians 4:6). In John's Gospel and letters, this idea occurs frequently, for example, "God is love. Anyone who lives in love lives in God and God lives in him" (1 John 4:16). So how do we talk to the modern adult about God?

- By starting at the feet of Jesus—not Plato's or Aristotle's.
- By examining his kingdom of God project which prioritized love of God and neighbour as a way in to a meaningful life.
- By opening our receptors to the presence of Jesus' Father, that is, the Transcendent, not only in Jesus himself, but in ourselves as well.
- By growing into the mindset of habitually living our daily lives in that presence.

There was another point which I made my own during my research. The Hebrew scriptures and Jesus himself experienced God as a close Presence. No pictures or statues, please! As the gospel spread to areas with a classical Greek culture, God came to be experienced in a different way. Paul's speech in the Areopagus (Acts 17:22–34) indicates his method: make Jesus' message relevant to his hearers' way of thinking. Early Christian apologists like Justin Martyr, Tatian and Polycarp did the same. No need to prove the existence of God—just demonstrate that Jesus is his son. In time, pictures and statues began to appear depicting Jesus' Father. That Father was assumed to live on the top deck of a double-decker universe, much in the same way as the disciples of Aristotle imagined the residence of the Supreme Being—in other words far removed from the close Presence that Jesus had preached.

The God of Jesus had been launched back into space! From being experienced as a loving Presence, he had now become a distant object of metaphysical speculation. His statues began to make him appear every inch a Roman Emperor, or King or other powerful figure. A nineteenth-century window in Holy Trinity Church in Chipping Norton (Oxfordshire) even has God the Father wearing a papal tiara! The current popular image of God is influenced by this historic caricature. Dewart would say that it contributed to the Death-of-God controversy of the 1960s. It certainly gets in the way when we try to revisit Jesus' own words about his and our Father.

As I completed my thesis, I had the feeling that I had resolved my lifelong problems with God. At least for the present.

How Life Light started

It was a hot, sleepless midsummer night of the summer of 1973. A week earlier I had read in *The Tablet* that the Corpus Christi Pastoral Centre in London, the only Catholic institution of its kind in England, was threatened with closure. This was bad news for adult religious education in the UK.

The Corpus Christi Centre had been running only since 1965. In January of that year the Provincial of the Sisters of Sion offered John Carmel Heenan, Archbishop of Westminster, some school property in Bayswater that was surplus to the Sisters' requirements. The main motivation was to put clergy, teachers and laity in touch with the new perspectives of Vatican II. Archbishop Heenan was initially very enthusiastic. With the help of Lumen Vitae, the new institute was up and running by the autumn term of the same year. The Principal was Hubert Richards, with Peter de Rosa as Vice-Principal. Full-time course participants numbered around a hundred, while extra-mural evening sessions attracted interested folks in very much larger numbers. Clearly there was a need here to be satisfied.

Several members of staff at Lumen Vitae were disappointed at the news of the possible closure. Some, like the Jesuit Marcel van Caster, had personally helped set up Corpus Christi. Others were regular visiting lecturers. They constantly quizzed me about the whys and wherefores of the closure. At the time I did not know; all my information came via my weekly *Tablet* which they avidly devoured. I could only speculate that the general line in theology being taken at Corpus Christi was more or less the same as that which I was appreciating so much at Lumen Vitae, and that this affair was inspired by resistance to change on the part of the higher echelons of Church authority. The Cardinal refused to agree to the list of visiting lecturers which the College had submitted to him. This list included some names from Lumen Vitae, although, up to the point when I left Brussels after my course, they had not been personally notified. The rejection of the list produced a reaction: all the Corpus Christi staff resigned.

I speculated on what could in practice be done to continue the work of Corpus Christi. There was an obvious need and it was clear that there were current difficulties in satisfying that need.

A possible project took shape in my mind on that hot summer night, the confluence of two personal experiences. The first was my working towards that London University degree at Hawkstone by means of Wolsey Hall Correspondence Courses. The second was the course I was about to complete at Lumen Vitae in Adult RE. Why not take a selection of Lumen Vitae modules, realize them into a UK setting, and then set up a correspondence course on the Wolsey Hall model?

No . . . I couldn't sleep!

I shared my thoughts with my Father Provincial (Charles Shepherd) in two letters; in the second I spelled out in some detail what I had in mind. I also sought advice from some members of the teaching staff at Lumen Vitae. After initial doubts about the effectiveness of distance learning—"learning only happens in a face-to-face setting!"—they became very supportive of my project and provided practical help in a number of ways.

In recognition of this I eventually named the project "Life Light".

5

Hawkstone Hall Correspondence Courses

The Hawkstone Pastoral Centre

In the summer of 1973, I returned to the UK from Brussels. On my arrival, I learned that I had been appointed to Hawkstone to help Father Seamus McManus set up a Pastoral Centre there, following the transfer of the seminarians to Canterbury. Some years earlier, as a member of the Formation Commission, I had recommended that the seminarians move from Hawkstone and that the empty seminary should become a Pastoral Centre. So, I was very happy with this appointment. In particular, I discerned in it the possibility of taking my "Life Light" project a stage further.

Jim McManus (as he was known at the time) had been a lecturer in moral theology at Hawkstone. He was now staying on to undertake the conversion of an enclosed seminary into a Pastoral Centre. The immediate task was to tidy up after the students' departure and refurbish the property. With astonishing rapidity, the spartan dispositions of an enclosed monastery were transformed into something resembling a hotel. All the bedrooms were now carpeted, lounge furnishings were softened, a bar was installed and much more. I personally converted the room of the Father Prefect of students at the end of the south wing into a library.

I mentioned above how I once went for the best part of a year at Hawkstone without consciously encountering a female. All now suddenly changed! Beryl Ruth, a professional caterer and author, took over in the kitchen. A number of Sisters from a variety of congregations became full-time members of the community, together with others who came and went in accordance with short-term projects. They were not engaged in domestic duties (as in past ages): they now led learning sessions, were involved in administration and generally kept us men in order! During my time at Lumen Vitae, I had gradually become accustomed to a kind of mixed community life, and so I was ready for this change to the Hawkstone community. However, for many other confreres, who were experiencing for the first time this transition from the old monastery to the new hotel, it was quite a sudden and dramatic change.

The new Pastoral Centre needed, of course, a steady flow of participants in a variety of day, week or longer courses to replace the recently departed seminarians. Jim and I quickly outlined a plan. Jim would set up a series of three-month residential courses, initially to meet the needs of priests and religious looking for an updating of their scriptural and theological literacy. These courses proved very successful and continued uninterruptedly until 2017.

I then discussed with him my ideas for a new project: a correspondence course based at our new Centre. In 1971, the Open University (OU), based in Walton Hall, Buckinghamshire, had accepted its first students. Its model of tuition was distance learning integrated with short residential periods, usually at other university campuses. I suggested to Jim that we adapted this OU model of tuition to my own project. Course participants could follow modules by correspondence course at home, and then join their peer-group at Hawkstone for discussion, liturgy and socializing.

I joined a small group from Belgium, Australia and elsewhere at Walton Hall to learn about OU administration of distance learning. At the end of this session, each of us was invited to submit an outline of administration for our own particular projects. These were examined and suggestions were then made. Based on these, I drew up my own system—and we have used it (more or less) ever since.

The first modules

I composed page 1 of Unit 1 of the first module of the new correspondence course on 1 September 1973. The module in question was The Church (Module 4 of the current *Certificate in Religious Studies* (CCRS) course). Over the next two years, and with the help of a number of confreres, I produced the first seven modules (to be described below). Each module comprised six or seven work units. They followed a pattern of programmed learning where one area of reflection leads smoothly into the next one. There was no attempt to design a logical progression of the modules themselves; each was intended to stand alone. Each module was accompanied by a course book with which the course material interfaced closely.

Alongside writing course material I advertised widely in the Catholic press, and I also circularized all the Catholic bishops of England and Wales, together with most of the Superiors-General of religious orders. Every one of the bishops replied—all of them very encouragingly. The first reply came by return of post from Bishop Derek Worlock of Portsmouth. The longest and warmest response came from Cardinal Heenan himself, who remembered me from PGCE days in Liverpool. There was an enthusiastic response from the Sisters too.

I was very encouraged when Redemptorist Publications at Chawton, Hampshire, indicated that they would like to be involved in the project. They offered to supply the course books and help with the designing and printing of the course material.

The plan was coming together at enormous speed! Jim designed a logo for the Hawkstone Hall Pastoral and Study Centre, and another one for Hawkstone Hall Correspondence Courses.

The first enrolments—clergy

The first enrolment, in February 1974, was from a priest in the archdiocese of Cardiff. This was quickly followed by other members of the clergy, a bishop, and (which is what I really welcomed) a number of confreres from the province.

The plan was to proceed in stages, in accordance with what we perceived as the most pressing sets of needs. The first of these was to provide priests with an opportunity to study Vatican II and its implications. This was to take the form of a course of In-Service Training. Drawing upon content from Lumen Vitae course material, by the summer of 1974 I had designed three modules—The Church, Catholic Theology since 1800 and Hermeneutics. Why these three? We tried to start from where potential course participants actually were. In this particular case this was seen to be clergy who were (obviously!) very closely involved in church matters; hence a module on the workings of the Church as an institution. The second module would address a commonly expressed misconception, namely that "all these changes" had happened as a result of shenanigans at Vatican II. The need here was to show how most of the insights articulated during the Council could be traced back to the mid-nineteenth century and beyond. The third module tackled the most challenging change of all—the new theology of Revelation.

The first in-service programme started in November 1974. Three dioceses (Cardiff, Shrewsbury and Menevia) applied to have their 1974–5 In-Service Training based upon this programme. The April 1975 residential section of the programme was attended by thirty-one clergy and two bishops. It was a lively session! The course evaluations were most encouraging.

The Sisters

The second stage of development aimed to address the needs of religious priests, sisters and brothers. Comparable to the programme for priests, I set up, with the help of Father Gerry Mulligan (lecturer in scripture), a three-module course of home-study and a short residential. We used The Church module. Gerry composed an eight-unit module on the Gospels which we later used more widely for a number of years. I put together a module on the Theology of Religious Life, based heavily upon Tillard's course at Lumen Vitae.

Why these three? These three modules, each in their own way, provided reassurance about the new setting in which religious were seeing themselves: no longer as a race apart from and above the generality of humankind, living a life which followed three evangelical counsels of poverty, chastity and obedience, but rather as communities of men and women who, among other things, gave witness to the values of the gospel in the Church and the world. Hence the three modules: The Church, The Gospels, and Religious Life. This programme proved more popular even than the clergy in-service programme. A large number of Sisters started working through these modules in their convents. (Some elderly Sisters insisted on plain envelopes!)

At the first residential there was not a spare room in the Hawkstone Centre. It was a very lively four days! There was a refreshing frankness and openness—especially among the Sisters. Some later admitted that they had spoken openly about some concerns for the very first time. One concern was the ageing and declining numbers of Sisters and the sadness that this was causing. "We care for fewer and fewer patients these days, and we are not being replaced by novices ... Our schools are gradually being taken over by lay-teachers ... We were founded to teach the children of poor parents and we are now teaching children of the rich. We have never had so few headmistresses ... What does the future hold for us?"

I prepared and delivered a session to share reflections on these issues. My main concern was to help the Sisters see these developments within the broader perspective of history. I suggested that there was an evolutionary pattern of development here. How much in our everyday lives has a religious background? The Knights Templars of St John set up a 3,000-bed hospital in Jerusalem in 1099 for all the sick of the city. The Order continued caring for the sick for centuries; the St John Ambulance group take their name from the Order. The Convent-Hospitals of nineteenth-century France were one of the inspirations of Florence Nightingale. She and the Sisters of Mercy changed the history of medicine by their work in the Crimean War. The Daughters of Wisdom, the Little Sisters of the Assumption and many other congregations delivered medical care over a long period of time until the National Heath Service (NHS) of 1945 took over and developed enormously all that the Sisters had been doing for centuries. Job well done! Sister Marie Louise Trichet, Sister Marie de Jésus and all the other Congregation founders might well rejoice that all they had so heroically worked for in their lifetimes had achieved a success beyond their wildest dreams.

In the history of education Jean-Baptiste de la Salle dreamed of education for all in the seventeenth-century. He founded the French Christian Brothers in 1684 and even set up the very first known teacher training college. In his footsteps walked Sister Jane-Francis de Chantal, Sister Julie Billiart, Catherine McAuley[1] and many others who did much pioneering work to enable education especially for the poor. Eventually, the 1870 Education Act provided education for all. Job well done! Jean-Baptiste de la Salle's dream had come true. Sister Jane-Francis de Chantal, Sister Julie Billiart, Catherine McAuley and all Sisters involved in education can rejoice at the successful outcome of their life's work.

So to all who felt depressed by these modern developments in medicine and education I said, "Relax! Job well done! Let's look for other urgent and neglected areas of concern. Trust in God to look after what happens in the future."

There followed a *very* lively discussion!

The laity

The third stage reached out to the laity, including the great number of teachers who had begun to hear about Hawkstone Hall Correspondence Courses. In addition to some of the modules I used with the clergy and the Sisters, I produced from scratch a module entitled The Basics of Christian Believing. This drew on my Lumen Vitae thesis on how to talk to the modern adult about God. It provided the course participant with a period of structured reflection upon our experience of God, Jesus' preaching of the kingdom of God, and the Holy Spirit. This new module would eventually lead on to a choice of other modules—including some new ones on the Liturgy and Christian Morals. The liturgical adviser to the diocese of Shrewsbury helped with the Liturgy module. I also owe a debt of gratitude to Jim McManus with regard to the Morals module.

I wrote short pieces about all this in *The Tablet*, the *Catholic Herald* and the *Universe* newspapers, and we very quickly became known in Catholic circles. From the autumn of 1973, and especially after the first hundred enrolments, there were a number of enthusiastic and encouraging articles in the *Catholic Herald*,[2] the *Universe*[3] and the *Catholic Fireside*.[4]

And elsewhere

As these articles began to reach foreign parts, there was such a large interest in our courses overseas that we had to add an International Section to our administration. As well as enrolling individual students for Air-Mail tuition courses, we received proposals from Zambia, Ghana and elsewhere to work towards establishing local distribution centres of our course material. Father Adrian Smith, a White Father working in Zambia, organized the first of these, based in the local diocesan seminary. Similar interest arrived from Victoria University and Auckland Catechetical Centre in New Zealand, Malaysia, Colorado USA, India (Kalugumalai and Secunderabad), Zimbabwe, Sierra Leone, Gibraltar, Australia, Addis Ababa, Nigeria, Canada, the Philippines, Lebanon and elsewhere. The initial letters followed a similar pattern: "We have needs here which I think could be met by your 'correspondence course + short residential' formula. Can we get together?"

Another use for our courses came from HM Prison Service. Our first such student enrolment was serving a sentence in Wandsworth, our second in Magilligan, followed by several others. (It was understood that any residential component would be wholly inappropriate!)

To facilitate journeys to and from Hawkstone Hall, I entered into negotiations with National Travel, an amalgamation of coach companies across the UK. After a surprisingly small amount of letter-exchanging we became a booking agency. This enabled us, at the same time as making reservations for our guests at Hawkstone, to send them return travel tickets to their home addresses. This proved quite convenient. A National Travel route passed the end of the drive. (I failed to get a request stop placed there, despite much trying!)

An open community

In addition to the three-month courses and our correspondence-course students, we were keen to attract other guests as well—chiefly as a means of raising some cash; in the early days we did not have too much of this! We advertised an "Open Christmas". The idea here was to welcome single individuals to join the community for as much or as little of the Christmas and New Year season's festivities as they wanted. Redemptorist Christmasses were traditionally very joyous and happy occasions with much spiritual and material feasting. We attracted some interesting and well-known personalities, such as Frank Field MP. We quickly formed a short-term close community and had a most spiritually fulfilling and festive time.

In the early days, we welcomed all sorts of groups and individuals. Charismatic groups loved the Hawkstone setting. They were the liveliest groups! Some guests came for holiday breaks, others for a few days of complete silence and solitude. On one occasion, however, there was a most unfortunate clash of interest. A Sister had booked in for a strictly silent retreat. And the local hunt was booked in to have their annual Hunt Ball on one of Sister's days—and nights! She was very understandably upset. "Disappointed" was the term she used, as I recall. We polished up our booking arrangements, and this never happened again.

A great start!

All in all, the new Pastoral Centre and Hawkstone Hall Correspondence Courses had got off to a good start. Jim had worked indefatigably, and his efforts had met with great success. The Centre began to look as if it had a future—and possibly a bright future as well. Jim had laid the foundations for a Centre which, over a period of some forty years, was to provide highly valued courses in spiritual renewal. Meanwhile the correspondence courses had exceeded all expectations. Within eight months of receiving our first enrolment from the priest in Cardiff we enrolled our hundredth participant in October 1974. But there were problems.

Problems

Earlier that same year I received a letter from the Provincial, Father Charles Shepherd. In it he required that all Hawkstone Hall correspondence course material be subjected to censorship by a board of three censors. For this task he appointed Fathers Gerry Mulligan, Jim McManus and Michael McGreevy. I had no problem with this. Gerry was a course writer himself; Jim was familiar with the content of all the modules; and Mick McGreevy was an old schoolmate of mine from St Philip's Grammar School in Birmingham. In the event, Gerry and Jim never raised a single point of concern. Mick spent a lot of time on the course material and made a few useful observations which were very helpful and for which I expressed my grateful thanks.

I was chatting about all this one day with another member of the Hawkstone community, Father Gerard Sugden. A Doctor of Canon Law, he had been my lecturer in Canon Law when I was a student. He expressed surprise that the question of censorship had arisen at all. It was only actual *books* that were subject to censorship. Correspondence course material pertained to the nature of correspondence, that is *letters.* No censorship was required. So what were we dealing with here? I was soon to discover!

The Centre bursar let it be known that Father Shepherd was worried about what the bishops would think of all this; he wanted the courses to be shut down. At the time, I was so immersed in the writing of course material and much else that I did not follow this up. I thought that this was just idle chat and perhaps the fruit of private speculation. In any case, I had had a very encouraging response from all the bishops, including Cardinal Heenan, and Father Shepherd knew this. He spent a fortnight at Hawkstone during the summer of 1975 and never mentioned any problems.

But then other developments began. Redemptorist Publications indicated that they were pulling out of the cooperation previously promised. Later *Catholic Life* magazine, which was published from Chawton, began a postal-tutored correspondence course based upon material published in the monthly magazine. (This course contributed much to adult RE. It closed in 1979 with the closure of the magazine. A fair number of *Catholic Life* course participants transferred to Life Light at the end of their courses.)

Father Shepherd was a long-standing friend of my family, and one of the many priests who had shared Mum's Sunday afternoon high teas. He had been in the same year as Uncle Chris throughout their noviciate and priestly studies. He was softly spoken at all times, enjoyed a reputation for holiness and was widely appreciated for the quality of his spiritual direction. He hated confrontation in whatever form it presented itself, preferring always to opt for the status quo. I would, however, have wished that communications between us during this period could have been better. I cannot count the number of sleepless nights I endured as I contemplated an uncertain future. Quite simply, if I did not have the support of the Provincial, the courses could not continue in their current form. I was, after all, a member of a religious community.

Obedience had got in the way of Hawkstone Hall Correspondence Courses.

How postal tutors started

During this time of uncertainty, I made some changes. With the possibility of being unable to welcome course participants to Hawkstone, I introduced postal tutors into the format. At the outset the first clerical participants worked through their courses by means of reading texts and then discussing them during the residential. There were no essays to be written. The same pattern was used for the Sisters and laity.

From Easter 1975, new course participants were no longer offered the possibility of residential sessions. Instead, each worked entirely at home with the help and continuous support of a postal tutor. I drew up a short programme of training for these tutors, which remained in use for many years. At first, the tutors were all priests and Sisters, later they were mostly all lay. The residential sessions had always been labour intensive and as they wound down, I found that I had more leisure time. I even took my first holiday in ages!

Solutions

In fact, it was a working holiday. The Redemptorist Fathers at St Joseph's in Brussels organized a weekly Mass for English-speaking Catholics, and they had asked for a locum to cover the period when the Irish Franciscan Father who usually celebrated this Mass would be away on vacation in August.

It was a great joy to breathe Belgian air again! I had the opportunity to revisit many of my old haunts in and around Brussels, as well as the Ardennes, Verviers, Leuven, Bruges and of course Lumen Vitae itself. I travelled everywhere by train with one of those go-where-you-like tickets. I always think more clearly when travelling by train!

And I really did do a lot of thinking, that summer of 1975, looking for solutions to the problem of my project. It had become clear that Hawkstone Hall Correspondence Courses could not continue at Hawkstone if the powers-that-be wanted them shut down. I had invested so much time and effort into these courses over the previous three years. Could I abandon the whole thing? Could I let down all those to whom I had promised so much? Who else would effectively address the needs of the moment?

No . . . the courses had to continue—somehow or other. But this meant that I would have to begin the process of leaving the Redemptorists—which I really did not want to do. In 1966 my brother Tony had made this move, following problems in the Chawton community. He had previously done great work there. He played a large role in pioneering the now-familiar Sunday Parish News bulletin, featuring Mass details on one side of an A4 sheet with space for parish notices, etc. on the other. He did late-night epilogues for nearby Southern Television in Southampton. (Tony was once cautioned over this—he was routinely breaking the Great Silence!) He eventually joined the Northampton diocese as a secular priest. He was given his first parish (St Clare's, Aylesbury) after the mandatory three-year period of "incardination" and a few years as a curate.

I had spent hours trying to dissuade him from taking this step. Now I too was facing something of Tony's problem. If I now followed the path that Tony took in 1966, could I continue with my project? (I was later to learn that it would be highly unlikely that any diocese would countenance anyone running a business during incardination.)

What about seeking admission to another religious order? I had come to love the Belgian Jesuits—but the Society of Jesus (quite rightly too) never accepts any priest from elsewhere. Moreover, the chances of being allowed to run a business during the noviciate of *any* religious order would be even less likely than being allowed to do so during incardination!

There remained the only other logical option: could I continue the work as a layman? My initial instincts gave me a clear answer—no! It would be a question of credibility. A priest at that time still had automatic credibility: once ordained, people listened. With laicization credibility would just as automatically depart.

Change of train—change of thought. For centuries, Catholic spirituality had come from the monasteries. As we were told in the noviciate, the idea was to spread the spiritual benefits and insights of one's prayer life to the faithful; in the case of the Redemptorists this was principally through parish missions. More intense lay spirituality was often modelled on monastic life: think of the Third Orders of St Francis, St Dominic, St Augustine and the Oblates of St Benedict. With the fresh vision of Vatican II, could the People of God as a whole, including especially the laity, credibly develop programmes specifically of *lay* spirituality? Courses in adult religious education *could* perhaps be perceived to acquire enhanced credibility by virtue of the very fact of originating in a lay setting.

I recalled a Vatican document of 1971[5] which portrayed Jesus as the "perfect communicator" because "he utterly identified himself with those who were to receive his communication. He gave his message not only in words but in the whole manner of his life. He spoke from within. He adjusted to his people's way of talking and to their patterns of thought." I reflected that that degree of identification of Jesus with his people was greater than mine, greater than that of many priests and theologians who (at the time) had to live somewhat apart from the mainstream of ordinary human experience. How often had well-meaning seekers after enlightenment at Hawkstone and elsewhere said to me after a conference: "Bless you, Father! All that sounds fine. But when you're married and with children, well . . . it's a bit different!"

A Christian mindset and way of life that was rooted in the gospel, mediated no longer via the cloister but via the hearth,[6] which recognized the holiness of daily living, which prized the married couple as God's close co-creators of new life, which brought comfort and support to them, and to all—this, I thought, was how the next stage of my project could be.

I am describing here with misleading brevity reflections which in fact covered a much longer period of time and many hundreds of train miles. There is a railway line that is very special to me, between Jemelle and Liège (since closed). It was while travelling this line that I took the decision to leave the Redemptorists and somehow or other to push ahead with my courses.

I returned to the UK after my holiday. On the coach between Ramsgate and London, which connected with the hovercraft from Calais, we passengers were being entertained by National Travel with easy-listening music. Karen Carpenter sang "Solitaire": "There was a man, a lonely man . . . While life goes on around him everywhere . . . And by himself it's easy to pretend, he'll never love again . . . , And solitaire's the only game in town . . . he's playing solitaire."

At the time, I mistakenly thought the Carpenters were "Mr and Mrs". I thought these were Karen Carpenter's own lyrics. Decades later I learned the truth: the Carpenters were brother and sister, the lyrics were written by Philip Cody, and Karen herself was having enormous health problems which eventually led to her untimely death. But I remember this occasion vividly. I became eye-wateringly emotional. It was as if God was communicating with me through the medium of Karen. I began to wonder if God was communicating to us all the time through the medium of everything around us.

The end of Hawkstone Hall Correspondence Courses

I informed Jim McManus of my decision at the end of October. At the same time, I informed Gerry Mulligan, who had now been elected as Provincial Superior to replace Father Charles Shepherd. Both Jim and Gerry were incredibly understanding and helpful in every way. Jim allowed me to keep the very large number of books which I had used to write the first modules—an enormously generous gesture! In return I undertook to continue with all my existing commitments until the laicization process was completed. I will never be able to thank Fathers Mulligan and McManus enough.

Telling Mum and Dad was something I had been dreading. Mum just quietly replied, "Oh dear!" and looked hurt. I wanted to talk her through my decision, but she constantly changed the subject and re-assumed her hurt look. I had more success with Dad over a pint. Tony's reaction was also supportive and very positive. He immediately drove down from Aylesbury to Hordle in Hampshire to help Mum through what he realized would be a difficult time for her. John, my other brother, was in contact too. After the conclusion of Tony's efforts, John summed up the situation: "Now you're *both* in the sh*t!"

Mum was very sensitive to fellow parishioners' opinions of my decision. She had always been very proud to inform all and sundry that "I have two sons who are priests!" When Tony left the Redemptorists, she wanted to leave the Abbey parish as quickly as possible. After Dad's retirement from work in 1966, they bought a bungalow in Hordle in Hampshire. Nearby a new Catholic parish was being established in Milford-on-Sea. The old Victoria cinema was tastefully converted into a church. Would Mum and Dad now feel that they had to move again? In the event, it was the Milford parishioners who gave Mum much genuine support and gently helped her to accept what had happened.

I completed all the application documents connected with laicization. I accomplished this rather time-consuming task with a heavy heart. I remained reluctant: part of me did not want to leave. For over a quarter of a century I had loved my life as a priest and Redemptorist. But I now had to make an act of faith in my future. With faith one can do things, and not do things, without fully knowing why.

My Dad died on 26 January 1976, aged seventy-four. Did agonizing over me have anything to do with his death? Mum always assured me that it did not. Tony thought otherwise. I tended to believe Tony. He was always closer to Mum than either John or myself, and I thought that he would know. Mum, as a true mother, could be economical with the truth if she thought it would promote happiness in the family or avoid distress.

My laicization document from the Vatican Congregation of Doctrine and Faith (CDF) is dated 2 April 1976. Father Mulligan asked me to leave Hawkstone and transfer temporarily to Clapham where laicization would be finally executed. The official procedure was that laicization took effect the moment that the Superior read out the CDF document to the applicant.

During June, I ran the correspondence course from Room 18 of St Mary's, Clapham. Each morning I would make my bed and pile up all the paperwork on top. Each evening I would put the lot back underneath my bed. Not a single course participant experienced any interruption of tuition—only a one-day postal delay through the redirection of mail.

These were the final days of Hawkstone Hall Correspondence Courses. They were also the lowest point of my life.

PART II

Life Light: The Flowering and Growth

This main part of the story climbs from that "lowest point of my life" into the refreshing regions of new and promising horizons. It was a slow climb at first. However, a number of new openings astonishingly presented themselves and the infant Life Light quickly learned to walk.

You will meet Heather. She would become not only my wife but also a major factor in the success of Life Light. Together we worked on what a lay spirituality might look like, endeavouring to construct a format that would sit as neatly upon the experience of ordinary everyday life as monastic spirituality related to the experience of religious life.

I hope that you will be struck by the large number of people who showed kindness and support to Heather and myself in our work for adult religious education. The received wisdom in the 1960s and 70s held that former priests were best advised to lie low after their laicization, and to get a job as far removed as possible from pastoral work and from their previous location. By contrast, you will see that a stream of encouragement came from University Colleges, Pastoral Centres, RE groups, Bishops, Clergy, Religious Priests and Sisters, as well as the laity.

You will see how Life Light came to be of service to teachers, as well as to the priests, religious and layfolk whom we originally set out to help. This has been mostly in connection with the Catholic Certificate in Religious Studies (CCRS) organized by the Board of Religious Studies of the Bishops' Conference.

Life Light Home Study Courses have a basically simple structure, though the details have changed over the near-half century of our existence in accordance with new circumstances and demands. I will describe the evolution of the courses, which will be of interest to the 13,000 course participants—but also, I hope, to the general reader as well.

Such a project has generated an enormous amount of study, reflection and writing. This in turn has produced a large feedback of insights, experience, wish-lists for the Church and society and—yes!—corrections. In my final chapter, I will share with you some of this accumulated resource, especially items which could be relevant to our immediate future as the members of the Catholic Church work synodically through the stages of the 2022–3 Roman Synod.

6

The Birth of Life Light

A fresh start

While running the course from my little bedroom in Clapham monastery, I was actively engaged in organizing my future and I was clear about what I had to do. I had to create a new environment in which to live and work. Like Jesus himself, I sought to adjust to people's way of life and to their patterns of thought, so as to be able to "post the Word" not only by using words but by the whole manner of my life—to speak from within.[1] I bought books on income tax, council tax and how to set up a small business, reflecting that Joseph and Jesus ran a carpentry business. They too would have been accustomed to taking and delivering orders, settling disputes, keeping their word, handling awkward customers, remitting the debts of bad payers, paying taxes, worrying about tomorrow—themes which would later feature in Jesus' Sermon on the Mount (cf. Matthew 5:23–6, 33–7, 39–42, 46; 6:25–34).

First, I had to find an affordable house and get a mortgage. The first task was easier than the second. I found an end-of-terrace, three-bedroomed property in Milton-under-Wychwood in West Oxfordshire. Milton was in many ways ideal for my purposes: a picturesque quiet Cotswold village which boasted essential amenities and (most importantly) a post office. It was situated within the Catholic parish of Holy Trinity, Chipping Norton, which at the time was being served by the Jesuits. There was a regular bus service. (There was little chance of my owning a car just yet!) Within the hour, I could access Oxford with all its relevant amenities, especially the Bodleian Library's Reading Room.

I applied to a local building society for a mortgage. I was firmly refused. As a self-employed trader I needed to show three years' accounts, which of course I could not do. To cut a long story short, I am eternally grateful to the Catholic Building Society, whose trustees went to a great deal of trouble. They examined in great detail my Hawkstone Hall Correspondence Course project. They concluded that the project was still promising, notwithstanding my changed circumstances. It was an act of faith on their part.

I moved into 7 Wychwood Drive in July 1976. I bought second-hand carpets and curtains, a refrigerator, a cooker, a table, a sideboard, a settee—all at knock-down prices. The family helped too. Mum contributed her fondue set and, most crucially helpful of all, Tony discovered in a corner of his presbytery a surplus-to-requirements hand-operated Roneo 250 duplicating machine. The largest bedroom became the Life Light office. My hundreds of books formed the wallpaper of the living room. My new neighbours in Wychwood Drive gave me an occasional hand with the heavier jobs.

In quiet reflective moments, I would contemplate the contents of my house. For the first time in my life, I actually owned these objects. Until recently my vow of poverty had forbidden me from owning anything. For me, even though I was now forty-one years of age, it was a totally new experience.

Surprisingly soon I was ready to resume running the correspondence courses. The first item on the agenda was to write a letter to every current student. Each one of these had enrolled with Hawkstone Hall Correspondence Courses. Each one had to be told of the changes—my laicization, the change of address and our new name. Not unreasonably, Father Mulligan had requested a name change. As a grateful recognition of my indebtedness to Lumen Vitae, I chose "Life Light".

It was an absurdly long letter; it ran to six pages! In it I detailed a selection of my reasons for making my decision. With the benefit of hindsight and if I could do a rerun of this episode, this letter would be considerably shorter: "This is what has happened/sorry for the inconvenience/you can have a full refund."

Replies and reactions came back almost by return of post. Not a single student who chose to reply was negative, not one discontinued their courses, not one requested a refund. All the responses were extremely sympathetic and understanding. Some of them were touching, like the

Sister from a South London primary school who had a whip-round in her school for me and enclosed a five-pound note with her reply! Her thoughtful kindness was the more touching by virtue of the fact that, at the point when her five pounds arrived, I really did need them—all five of them! During those first few months I entered fully into the experience of large sections of humanity who do not have the wherewithal to make ends meet.

The joys of self-employment

There are a number of economic models for financing business start-ups. Most often one secures a loan from a bank. With this one pays for all the various items needed to set up a business. As the first orders come in and the first invoices get paid, the loan is gradually repaid out of profits, often over a considerable period of time.

My visit to the Small Trades Advisory Service office was not terribly promising. The chap who interviewed me saw few prospects for a correspondence course in denominational theology organized by an ex-priest! My bank took a similar line, wondering how I would be in a position to keep up with my repayments—especially if I also had a mortgage.

You may recall Jimmy Mythen asking me a decade earlier to run an O level economics course in the Juvenate. One topic in that course now came back into my mind: the business model used by "Tom".

"Tom" was a young fourteen-year-old with a mind for business. He took an early morning job delivering newspapers for £10 a week. At the end of each week, he would split his earnings into two: he would spend £5 on himself, and he would put £5 into the bank. By the end of his first year, he had saved £250. With this he bought a second-hand bike which enabled him to deliver twice as many papers. His salary increased to £20 per week, which he spent and saved in the same way. In this way he accumulated £500 by the time he was sixteen, £1,000 by the time he was seventeen, and £1,500 by the time he was old enough to drive a car. He now set himself up in business offering a range of services to senior citizens at £10 a visit. He eventually became quite wealthy.

I followed Tom's business start-up model: I would expand out of profits. I would adhere to a very tight budget. Among my memorabilia I still have a small book in which I wrote down every item of household expenditure, as a means of cutting my outgoings to a bare minimum.

Of course, unlike Tom, I was not starting from *absolute* scratch. I had the course participants who had enrolled at Hawkstone and who were loyally continuing. I had a comfortable amount of course books which I would be able to sell in due course. I had already acquired the various items needed to start running Life Light. But things were still really tight.

A significant difference from my time at Hawkstone was that I was not in any financial position to commission new modules. One urgent need of the moment was to produce a module on the Liturgy. There were a host of changes happening to the way Mass was now being celebrated, and people wanted to study the background to them. From Hawkstone I had contacted a number of recognized authorities to see whether they would be willing to help produce course material: Kevin Donovan, Brian Newnes, J. D. Crichton and Clifford Howell SJ. All expressed sincere enthusiasm and encouragement; however, none had the leisure time needed to be of help. Father Howell was particularly touching. Having turned me down, he wrote again a fortnight later. He had experienced much remorse at having turned me down, so he sent me pages and pages of really useful material.

I concluded that the only way forward was to write the module myself, based upon the Lumen Vitae course on Liturgy. This way I could get the module out more quickly, and I would not have to pay anyone.

I was wearing a multiplicity of hats. Whereas at Hawkstone I had members of the team to look after the administration, produce course material, send out the weekly postings and so on, in my new setting I had to do everything myself. Moreover, there were now income tax returns, council tax paperwork, gas and electricity bills, front and back gardens to maintain, and the immediate need to teach myself to cook.

"Tom" would have been proud of me! By the end of August 1976, I had enough cash to pay for a series of Life Light advertisements in *The Tablet* and the *Catholic Herald*. On 17 September the first Life Light enrolment form arrived—from Maureen Duckworth.

Introducing Heather

Did Heather have anything to do with my decision to leave the Redemptorists? She always maintained that she did not!

It is time to introduce Heather.

Heather Farr was the only daughter of Noreen and Harry Farr. Noreen was born in Bonniconlon, Co. Mayo, Harry in Widnes, Cheshire. The family retired to Hordle in Hampshire around the same time as my own Mum and Dad retired there too. Our two families struck up a friendship, and we spent many happy hours together in each other's homes.

Heather was educated with the Canonesses Regular of St Augustine in their boarding school in Rise, Yorkshire. She then went to the University of Hull where she read theology, and immediately afterwards transferred to St Hugh's College, Oxford, from where she obtained her Postgraduate Certificate in Education (PGCE).

It was during her final year at Hull that we found that we were spending increasing amounts of time together "discussing theology". She even visited Hawkstone during 1975 to get to grips with Teilhard de Chardin. At this stage, she was just a friend of the family. But that was to change!

To earn extra cash, she worked during her vacations at the nearby New Milton library. On one occasion, I went into her library when it was quiet and devoid of clients. I approached her at the reception desk. "Do you have anything on the religions of the Upper Brahmaputra region?" (How about that for a chat-up line?)

She didn't chat. Professionally she led me to the spirituality section—a rather secluded corner of the library. Together we rather pointlessly scanned titles on the spines of hard-backed books. After a little while, she turned and gently smiled. She accepted my invitation to lunch at the Red House Hotel in Barton-on-Sea.

When I told my folks of my decision to leave the Redemptorists, I told Heather and her family as well. I subsequently received a most sympathetic and understanding letter from Harry and Noreen which I found very reassuring.

Heather was nineteen years my junior—but the age gap never seemed to matter. From the start we had so much in common. Heather and I had long and deep discussions about theology, changes in the Church, current affairs, and also religious life, about which she was very knowledgeable. While at Hull, she had for a time thought of joining the Canonesses of St Augustine, and the Sisters gave this one-time Head Girl at Rise much encouragement. While at Hawkstone, she bumped unexpectedly into Sister Gabriel, who would have been her novice mistress. Later Sister Alexia, one of her teachers and lifelong friend, joined us on Oxford station for a chat. She and Heather reminisced about old times at Rise until our train arrived. Years later, Alexia revealed that she had in fact been sent by the Sisters at Rise to split us up!

Did I have anything to do with her change of mind? I always maintained that I did not.

Something wonderful

Time passed, and Heather and I met with increasing frequency. One such get-together was very special.

We had planned a weekend in York. After a somewhat uncomfortable bus journey from Hull—a young child threw up in the seat next to us—we booked into the Lady Anne Middleton Hotel. I carried Heather's case into her room, and we talked. Somewhere between 1.30 and 3.00 in the afternoon I recall making a long, amorous monologue. Suddenly I felt inspired to drop to my knees. "Heather, darling . . . will you marry me?" At that moment something wonderful happened, which I shall try to describe.

Blood rushed to my head. There was a flashback to the path beyond the rose garden in Hawkstone, followed by a feeling of calm—as when the sun breaks through a cloudy sky, or when one reaches the end of a journey. For what seemed to *me* an age she did not reply. My heart was just beginning to sink when she gently and breathily vocalized the sweetest word I will ever hear—"Yes!"

I had no engagement ring! This had not been on my agenda. She wore a pearl ring on a finger of her right hand. She now transferred it to her left.

We often talked about this in the years that followed. We frequently compared our two versions of what occurred. You have just had my account. *Hers* went something like this:

"Suddenly you went on your knees and said 'Darling, I love you. Will you marry me?' I said, 'Yes. What kept you? Are you alright?'"

Heather always insisted that she said her "yes" immediately. My own perception was that she delayed. Which made us wonder . . .

Some couples go to great lengths to create a setting suitable for "popping the question"—on a gondola on a canal in Venice, on the top of the Eiffel Tower, on a bridge in Manhattan . . . On the other hand, the French Catholic philosophers Jacques and Raïssa Maritain were one evening discussing a point of philosophy when Jacques suddenly adopted the approved kneeling position and proposed. Raïssa agreed. Whereupon they resumed their seats and continued their discussion from where they left off!

As for us, my diary reads: "It just happened! I would have planned it differently (perhaps I plan too much!), but now I would not have wanted it to have happened in any other way." I had spent two years of my seminary days at Hawkstone in search of mystical experience (see Chapter 2). If what I have just related is in any way describable as a spiritual experience, it certainly came without my asking.

We saved our official engagement announcement until later. On Christmas Eve 1976, I asked Harry for his daughter's hand in marriage. Noreen, an accomplished goldsmith, had produced a spectacular engagement ring—18-carat gold with a large diamond inlaid in a daisy setting. I now slipped this on to Heather's finger, and we all went to Midnight Mass at St Francis of Assisi's Church in Milford-on-Sea.

It was in the same church that Heather and I got married on 15 July 1977, after she had completed her PGCE. Jimmy Mythen performed the ceremony and celebrated our Nuptial Mass. All the members of both our families were present. Mum had hesitated for a few months, but finally gave in to family pressure. On the day she looked quite radiant and happy. My brother John lent us one of his cars—a sporty-looking MG—and off we headed north next day to Dornie in Scotland for our honeymoon.

Boundless energy

Heather and I had led very busy lives during the year before we got married. She successfully worked through her PGCE course in Oxford, while I nurtured the infant Life Light. As for myself I experienced boundless energy.

Following contacts made at Hawkstone, I accepted an invitation to preach on the Catholic Charismatic Movement in All Saints Church of England church in West Bromwich. I also led an Anglican clergy two-day session at Shallowford House in Staffordshire on the Holy Spirit and the new rite of reconciliation.

Moreover, having completed the Liturgy module, I began researching a much-needed module on moral theology. The encyclical *Humanae Vitae* (1968) was causing problems for many thoughtful Catholics. They needed the opportunity to reflect on the broader picture of Catholic moral theology and upon possible alternative approaches to the issue of birth control. My diary for Wednesday 2 February 1977 communicates this high productivity level. "The second unit of *Christian Morals* got itself dispatched on time. I only started to type it on Monday. Between then and today I typed, duplicated, stapled, packed and posted it. I suppose that I shall one day look back at such feats with nostalgia!"

I do!

A husband-and-wife model

Back from honeymoon, I carried Heather over the threshold of our little house as tradition dictated. Thereafter the house transformed itself perceptibly into a home, with love in every room. My new experience of owning things underwent modification. *My* settee was now *our* settee!

We began to take decisions together. We never really successfully analysed how this process actually worked in our case—but we were happy that it actually did. We worked together as much as possible—decorating, cleaning, prettifying the garden—although she wanted to do rather more cooking than I did!

Heather also wanted to be involved in Life Light. She had already begun postal tutoring the module on the Gospels which Gerry Mulligan had written. She also gave a hand with administration until she began teaching RE at St John Almond's Secondary School in Banbury.

We never considered ourselves a "model husband and wife". However, we did set out to apply the husband-and-wife model to Life Light. I had been aware during my Hawkstone days that a few female course participants would have preferred the course materials to have been developed by women. We now had the possibility of meeting this challenge to some extent. With her theological background, Heather would critically review all new course material from a female point of view, so that the texts could be studied comfortably by women participants. As existing course material came up for revision, the same process would be applied.

An example of this process: the context is the Life Light module on Christology, at the point where we address the question "is God a 'He' or a 'She'?" Having demonstrated from the early chapters of Genesis that God was perceived as a reality that is neither male nor female but rather One that transcends both, we proceeded:

> The use of personal language about God involved a decision: would *male* personal pronouns or *female* personal pronouns be used? It had to be one or the other: at the time, people experienced persons as either male or female. There was no appreciation of multi-sexualities. For practical purposes male terminology was used. (Given the male-dominated character of Hebrew life, there probably was not a great deal of discussion!) However calling God a "He" was, strictly speaking, a convention.[2]

No prizes for guesssing Heather's input!

We later took this approach a stage further. Invited once to lead a session on "Catechesis in the home" at St Mary's, Strawberry Hill, we installed two lecterns and delivered the input section of the session much in the way that television news presenters were to read the news a few years later—with alternate male and female contributions.

Later still, when Life Light ran study weekends in Llandudno, Derry and Dublin as well as in St Mary's, whenever possible (that is, children permitting) we would co-present what we had on offer. In this way, we moved closer to the ideal of speaking the Word from out of the situation of ordinary folk—as Jesus himself did.

7

Working with St Mary's

How it started

In April 1977, Father Desmond Beirne, a Vincentian priest and newly appointed Principal of the University of London Institute of Education at St Mary's, Strawberry Hill, delivered a paper entitled "Key Problems in Religious Education". One of the problems he identified was the need for in-service training for teachers of RE. In-service courses were insisted upon by the then Department for Education and Science (DES) but rendered difficult by the reluctance of Local Education Authorities (LEAs) to release teachers for this purpose. Father Beirne's paper was summarized in an article of 22 April in the *Catholic Herald*.

I immediately wrote to Father Beirne. In my letter, I outlined a possible solution to the problem he had raised. To keep both the DES and the LEAs happy, could we not design an in-service course using the Open University model of home study plus a short residential, with St Mary's providing the residential element and ourselves delivering the home-study component? (This would be a continuation of the structure we set up in Hawkstone which had worked so well.) In this way, the DES would have the in-service courses they wanted, while the LEAs would not have to release their teachers for long periods.

My proposal was well received and earned me a splendid lunch in Walpole House.

St Mary's, Strawberry Hill

St Mary's has a splendid setting on the banks of the Thames near Twickenham in Middlesex. It has an impressive history. Horace Walpole (1717–97) was the son of Robert Walpole, the first Prime Minister of Great Britain. It was Horace who purchased Walpole House in 1749 and developed it so imaginatively that it is now internationally recognized as the first example of English Gothic Revival. He went on to write *The Castle of Otranto* here in 1764, the first Gothic novel. Lady Frances Waldegrave (1821–79) subsequently added an elegant wing to the house to enable her to entertain her many influential guests, which included William Wilberforce and William Gladstone.

In 1923, the estate was bought by the Catholic Education Council. St Mary's College, which had been founded in 1850 in nearby Hammersmith, transferred to Strawberry Hill in 1925. It was directed over several decades by the Vincentian Fathers, until Father Beirne's retirement in 1992. After periods of affiliation with the universities of London and Surrey, St Mary's became a university in its own right in 2014. It currently provides courses for about 6,000 students.

At our lunch, many possibilities were discussed, and in the light of them Father Beirne asked me to draw up a pilot plan. This was ready by early June, a few days before Heather and I got married. In it I described the aim of the new in-service programme as follows. "Making use of already-existing facilities available to St Mary's College and Life Light, to provide an 'open university' pattern of in-service training, designed to put teachers in touch with:

(a) recent thinking in the Church;

(b) recent methods of communicating within a school context our life of faith in Christ."

Life Light would undertake to provide learning-sessions which would address (a); St Mary's would deal with (b) during a summer school to be held in the first week of the summer vacation.

The scheme was discussed by the Religious Studies (RS) department of the College and subsequently by the RE Inspectorate of the DES. Following a wide circularizing of information about the new scheme, I received a great deal of interest and enthusiasm from, among many others, Norman St-John Stevas (Secretary of State for Education) and Kevin Nichols (RE Adviser to the Bishops of England and Wales). The Association of Teaching Religious Education ordered 1,000 sets of information about the course, while the Irish Secondary Schools Association circularized all their members.

The college appointed a link person for us, a recent graduate of Lancaster University. This was my first introduction to Daniel O'Leary, a young, vivacious priest of the Leeds diocese who was joining the RS department of St Mary's in September 1978, and who was to influence Life Light in many ways over the decades. (Daniel was known as "Donal" during the twentieth century. For simplicity's sake I will call him by the name he chose around the turn of the millennium.) He and I finalized the programme of the first of the summer schools which was held between 23 and 27 July 1979.

The summer schools

These schools, or later variants of them, were to run for some thirty years until 2009. As was our experience at Hawkstone, the members of the groups that came together following the period of their distance-learning studies were remarkable for the way in which they so promptly and so effortlessly gelled together. This was one of the many advantages of the "home study plus brief residential" format: each individual had much in common already with each other individual, including the experience of working through an identical set of course materials. As a result, almost upon arrival, the Life Light course participants formed a meaningful group of participants. Many of our speakers remarked upon this difference—how receptive they were and how easy to work with from the start.

The early years of the summer schools coincided with the period of enthusiasm for the charismatic movement. The friendly ethos of the Life Light groups was particularly evident in the liturgies. Daniel always aimed to provide a progressive and inspiring form of Eucharist. On occasions, these Masses would go on for hours! On one occasion after the liturgy of the Word, the Bidding Prayers went on rather too long for one elderly

Sister. She had prayed along with the group for over twenty minutes for everybody and everything from the pope to some endangered species of red squirrel. She was inspired to add one of her own: "That this be the last bidding prayer: Lord, in your mercy . . . ". And it was!

In the early days, most of the leaders of the various learning sessions were members of the RS department, notably Bernard Loughran, Duncan Macpherson, Mary Grey, Teresa Sallnow, Perry Gildea, Jim Alford, Michael Prior and Tony McCaffrey. In addition, Daniel succeeded in attracting a number of eminent contributors to successive summer schools: Kevin Nichols (author of *Cornerstones*, 1978), Bishop David Konstant (editor of *Signposts and Homecomings*, 1981), Patrick Purnell SJ (*Our Faith Story*, 1985; *To Be a People of Hope*, 1987), Mary Boys, Tom Groome (*Christian Religious Education*, 1980), Gabriel Moran (*Theology of Revelation*, 1966; *God Still Speaks*, 1967), John Elias (*The Foundations and Practice of Adult Religious Education*, 1982), John Hull (RE Director, Birmingham University), Brenda Watson (Farmington Institute) and Anne McDowell (founder of the Association of Adult Religious Educators).

I would now like to indicate how two in particular of these session leaders influenced the development of Life Light.

Introducing Shared Praxis

Tom Groome was the principal speaker at our 1984 summer school. It proved to be a significant event in the developing story of RE in these isles. Over three days he took us through his "Shared Praxis" approach to religious education, the subject of his *Christian Religious Education*. This was the occasion when he first introduced his new approach. As well as Life Light participants, there were many people taking part from home and abroad who had a responsibility for RE in their areas. In this way, most of the school RE programmes which appeared in the years that followed incorporated the main procedures of Shared Praxis.

Shared Praxis is the term which is used to describe a specific kind of Christian religious education, in which a group of Christians share in dialogue their reflections on their current attitudes, in the light of the

Christian story and of its vision—and this for the purpose of promoting a lived Christian faith. In Shared Praxis, there is an introductory focusing section, followed by five stages or "movements":

- Present Action
- Critical Reflection
- The Christian Story and Vision
- Dialogue between the Story and the participants' stories
- Dialogue between the Vision and the participants' visions.

Teachers who deliver RE programmes such as *Come and See*, *Alive O!*, *Grow in Love* or *Here I Am* will be familiar with these stages. The Life Light module *Introduction to Religious Education* has a whole section dedicated to Shared Praxis.

Incarnational Theology

Daniel O'Leary's own input to the 1982 summer school had, and continues to have, a deep effect upon many. His specific contribution is contained in *Love and Meaning in Religious Education* which he co-authored with Teresa Sallnow, and which was published by Oxford University Press in 1983. His further reflections, stimulated by Pope Francis' *Laudato Si!*, are very accessible in *An Astonishing Secret*, published by Columba Press in 2017.

It was during the 1982 summer school that Daniel introduced us to his ideas for RE. The new approach went by the name "Incarnational Theology". It is best appreciated when contrasted with our traditional way of thinking. According to this, our human race is a fallen race, following Adam and Eve's original sin in the Garden of Eden. The work of Jesus was seen to be a rescue mission. He came down from heaven, revealed God's plan for us and, as our Redeemer, paid the price for our sinfulness by his crucifixion, thereby restoring humankind. After his resurrection he ascended back into heaven, leaving his Church to carry on his work in his name and to offer salvation to all who would be baptized.

Daniel identified the problems which a number of theologians have with this account. Firstly, our knowledge of the cosmos has changed from the flat earth view of biblical times to our perspective of a universe of mind-boggling dimensions. The audience at a Coventry Mystery play in the fourteenth century thought of heaven as a place located up in the skies at no greater distance vertically than Kenilworth Castle, five miles down the road, was horizontally. Given this "double-decker universe", Jesus could credibly, if miraculously, have ascended there after his resurrection.

Secondly, the concept of original sin itself has been re-examined. It used to be thought that it was St Paul in his Letter to the Romans (5:12–20) who launched the idea of original sin. However, more recently it has become common to ascribe the origins of this concept to St Augustine of Hippo (354–430)[1] in trying to justify the practice of infant baptism. He thought that we had all sinned in Adam's act of disobedience, that the consequent guilt had passed down through the generations by sexual intercourse, and that consequently we could be labelled as a "fallen race". Parents had their infant children baptized to restore them to grace as soon as possible. So great was the authority of St Augustine that his conclusions influenced thinking throughout the Middle Ages and beyond, leading to, for example, the doctrine of limbo (widely thought to have been removed from theological consideration by Benedict XVI in 2007) and the doctrine of the immaculate conception of Mary, according to which she was exempted from incurring the stain of original sin in view of her future role as the mother of Jesus.

Thirdly, if Jesus paid the price of our redemption, to *whom* precisely did he pay the debt? To the devil, as Origen (c.185–c.254) wondered? To his Father? If the latter, does this not dramatically move our concept of God away from that portrayed by Jesus in the parables?

Incarnational Theology derives its name from the *incarnatus est* of John 1:14—"the Word became flesh and lived among us", which describes Jesus as the divine logos (Word), who has now become a member of the human race. According to Daniel's way of contemplating God, incarnation first took place at the moment of creation itself. God has been "in" his creations from the start and continues to be so. Throughout his ministry Jesus *revealed* God's closeness to us, rather than *inaugurated* it. His central message, the Reign of God, challenged us to abandon selfishness (the sin of the world) and lead lives of love—love of God and love of our neighbour. His crucifixion was the dramatic demonstration of just how unconditional that love and selflessness has at times to be. This was a vivid example of that very love and forgiveness for an enemy that Jesus had been inculcating a few months previously, offering no resistance to the wicked but rather turning the other cheek. A people that incorporates this mindset of unconditional love into its daily life will be saved.

In his 1982 sessions, Daniel provided the following table of contrasts between the traditional perceptions and the ones he proposed:

	Traditionally	**Proposed**
God	Out there	In here
Humankind	Fallen	Graced
Jesus as man	Superhuman	Human
Creation	Failed	Succeeded
Incarnation	A "Plan B"	The "Plan A"
Church	Separate from the world	The world itself
Sacraments	Things	Moments
Prayer	Saying	Being
Sin	An act against the law	An act against love
Original sin	Historical	Mythical

As I followed Daniel's lectures, I was conscious of how closely his proposals resonated with my own, as I had expressed in the final section of my Lumen Vitae thesis a decade earlier. But he was taking me further and, in the intervening years, I spent time thinking about this further mile. For want of a better place in this book, I would like at this point to outline a summary of my reflections.

Reflections on Incarnational Theology

Jesus revealed God's closeness to us, rather than inaugurated it. In support of Daniel's line of thinking here, the Hebrew scriptures often bear witness to ideas and concepts being subject to evolution; for example, the developing perceptions of Covenant and Wisdom.

The same pattern is discernible in the progressive appreciation of the closeness of God to humankind. God was perceived as a *Presence*, associated in a special though not exclusive way with the Ark of the Covenant, the wooden chest that contained the Jewish Law. Exodus 25:22 promises that "there I shall come to meet you". The Mosaic Law forbade graven images of God (Exodus 20:4–5)—a prohibition that prevented God from becoming an *object* of speculative thought, as happened later in Christian philosophy. This Presence was felt as a close presence; in Leviticus 26:11–12 God declares that he will make his abode among the people. "I shall live among you; I shall be your God and you will be my people." God is described by Jeremiah as using a term which was later to be seen as enormously significant: "for I am a *father* to Israel . . . they will all know me, from the least to the greatest" (Jeremiah 31:9 and 34). God is felt to be particularly close to the prophets, as when Elijah experienced God speaking through "a light sound of silence" on Mount Sion/Horeb (1 Kings 19:12), or more generally as they declare that "it is the Lord who speaks". That the presence of God could be felt intensely at a personal level is clear from Psalm 139: "O Lord, you search me and you know me. You yourself know my resting and my rising . . . ".

If it is true that God has been, and is, in his creation from the start, these and similar texts indicate a growing perception of this. They therefore go some way to support Daniel's affirmation that incarnation predates Jesus.

Jesus assumed his contemporaries' ideas on God but took them very much further. He talked about God not just as a knowing and reassuring God, but as a present and *caring* Father, on a scale not previously contemplated. Jesus' use of "Abba" when addressing the Father (as in Mark 14:36) is an indication, not only of how close Jesus knew God was to himself, but also of how close he knew God was to *all* of us (cf. Romans 8:15; Galatians 4:6). In John's Gospel and letters, this idea occurs frequently. For example, the author of the First Letter of John is even more explicit here: "Whoever keeps his [God's] commandments abides in God and God in that person" (1 John 3:24). "God is love, and whoever abides in love abides in God and God in him" (1 John 4:16).

When we think about the ways in which God may be present to us in our personal lives, we cannot but be struck by a number of Gospel passages which would seem to indicate that God is as close to us as our very life, in other words that God is *in* us. When Jesus warns us against parading our piety in Matthew 6:6, he tells us instead: "Go to your private room, shut yourself in, and pray to your Father who is in that secret place." The picture of God awaiting me in my private room is very vivid. Jesus himself prays privately in all sorts of places. "He would withdraw to deserted places and pray" (Luke 5:16)—not necessarily to special places—where his Father would be awaiting him. The implication is that God is with us always, whether we are walking down the street or engaging in any sort of activity, but is more palpably present to us when we retire to some place of quiet and self-open to that presence—as in prayer.

Another instance of this awareness of God's presence is Matthew 6:4, where Jesus promotes private almsgiving: " . . . and your Father who *sees all that is done in secret* will reward you". In terms of my personal experience, I alone have knowledge of what I have secretly done—good things or bad things. Jesus affirms on multiple occasions that God is privy to this knowledge, *my* knowledge. No closer presence than this can be imagined.

These passages help us to appreciate more fully references to God being also present in our neighbour. This idea is repeated many times in Matthew 25, where the sheep are being separated from the goats in the final judgement. "For I was hungry, and you gave *me* food . . . . In so far as you did this to the least of these brothers and sisters of mine, you did it to *me*" (Matthew 25:35–40). God is thus seen as being intimately present to everybody. It would have been uncharacteristic of Jesus to have made a distinction here between Jews and Gentiles, or male and female: if God is present to some, he is present to all.

When the gospel was later preached to people with a Greek educational background, they assumed that God was to be thought of in terms of

Aristotle's Supreme Being, and so this closeness of God which Jesus had demonstrated lost its emphasis. God became distant once more.

However, universal awareness of God in us is a widely felt experience. It is sometimes linked to our experience of conscience. In Hinduism, conscience is "the invisible God who dwells within us". Socrates was aware of a "divine monitor" within him. Seneca sees conscience as the voice of God within man.[2] The Hebrew scriptures did not have a word for "conscience". However, the writers identified the reactions of heart and loins in moral matters as the voice of God (cf. Psalms 7 and 25; Jeremiah 11:20; 17:10). Following Paul's thinking on conscience in Romans 2: 14–16, 1 Corinthians 10:24–29 and elsewhere, Christian theology traditionally saw conscience as "the voice of God for an individual and the real guarantee that his life is anchored in God and in the law of Christ".[3] We are all conscious of the "inner voice" within us. Frequent mentions of it are made in all sorts of settings, secular as well as religious. It may be that we routinely underestimate its significance.

At the launch of Daniel's book *Dancing with Death*, published after his death in January 2017, his literary adviser Margaret Sibery recalled that Daniel believed that the life, work and ministry of Jesus had the effect of embracing everything that is human in life and subsuming it into the divine. As a result, we can now contemplate God as "the love energy at the heart of our evolving universe and at the heart of our everyday lives .... (Now) we encounter God not *in* our life but *as* our life".[4] The first line of his *Astonishing Secret* reads as follows: "Once we equate God with life itself a transformation takes place in the way we believe." I have been much attracted to this equation and I would like to share with you the reasons why.

The God of Life

When we contemplate God there are two dimensions that impose themselves upon our awareness: the transcendent and the immanent.

First, there is the transcendent dimension: we are aware of God as beyond the furthest reaches of our limited minds. When researching for my Lumen Vitae thesis, I discovered that last century a number of theologians (Jürgen Moltmann, Wolfhart Pannenberg, Johann Baptist Metz, Leslie Dewart) expressed the view that transcendence should no longer be bracketed with metaphysics (as down the centuries) but rather with time and history—in keeping with the categories of thought in the Hebrew scriptures, and hence of Jesus himself. So let us bracket the Transcendent with what we know of our human history.

The Big Bang occurred 13.8 billion years ago, resulting in an ever-expanding, immeasurable universe. We live on one of the smaller planets in our galaxy. We are awestruck by the immensity of creation, and so of its awe-inspiring Creator. We emerged as a human race in Africa about 70,000 years ago. From there we slowly but surely spread all over the planet, reaching the Red Sea about 65,000 years ago and, millennia later, India, Europe, China and eventually the Americas. By 30,000 years ago, we had settled all over the earth. Civilisation appeared 3,000 years ago in Egypt.

In faith, we contemplate God's involvement at every stage in this story—every birth, nest-flitting, exploration, death—right up to our own day and to our own births, marriages and deaths. Each human is born, lives and dies. God, as the Transcendent, just lives. That is the difference between God and us.

I will die. God will live on. I too will live on in the sense that my children carry my genes and perhaps will pass them on to children of their own. Perhaps this ongoing generating will also continue for another 70,000 years or more. I will be seen in retrospect as having been an essential part of that ongoing history, just as, 65,000 years ago, some brave human negotiated the Red Sea out of Africa—an essential part of all our stories. I will therefore pass into that same history. I will therefore pass into the transcendent.

We can thus discern the involvement of the Transcendent in the process of evolution—not only human evolution, but all its other myriad forms. Teilhard de Chardin thought of God as the One who goes before us, educing the higher forms of evolution out of the lower ones. It was the insight of the Process theologians that discerned God as working from inside us.

Then there is the immanent dimension of our awareness of God. Which one of us has not at some point been overwhelmed by "the wonder of our being" (Psalm 139:14), how our various parts work together for our ongoing good health? We have seen how Jesus made us aware of the presence of God within ourselves, within nature, within our neighbour.

Why do we equate God with life? Life is immanent to each one of us as an individual: life also transcends us, and (in its totality) is beyond us in time and space. These two dimensions of God-awareness—transcendence and immanence—come together in the concept of Life. Life is as old as time itself, and as immense as the universe. Life is all around us and within us—as indeed Jesus said God is (cf. Matthew 6:4; 25:35–40).

The Hebrew scriptures are prefaced (cf. Genesis 1) with a dramatic proclamation that God is the "God of Life"—the most basic of all the titles that the scriptures gave to God. The title used most often is the YHWH of Exodus 3:14. This is variously translated but it seems to mean "he who brings into being whatever comes into being"—that is, the God of Life. This is the most fundamental of all God's titles. The Christian scriptures continue this theme and state that Jesus "came that (we) may have life, and have it in plenty" (John 10:10), and that at a deep level life is enriched if we follow Jesus. For these reasons, I would suggest that we examine Incarnational Theology and also the possibility of approaching the reality of God in terms of life. I have concluded that Daniel is justified in promising a new way of living out our faith once we approach God in this way.

From early on, Heather and I used to pray together the Evening Prayer of the *Prayer of the Church*. Later we substituted this practice for another: we would hold hands and be content to simply *be* together in the presence of the God of Life.

Yes, Heather and I owe much to the Head of RS at St Mary's!

Certificates

To return to a more mundane subject, teachers and others—but especially teachers—who had worked through both the home study and residential sections of our programme wanted a "piece of paper" to record their achievement. Life Light participants received the "Life Light Certificate in Adult Religious Education". The credibility of this document relied entirely upon the credibility of the course programme itself: it was too soon to think that Life Light of itself had much credibility!

Daniel, Teresa, Heather and I discussed this problem during the first two summer schools in 1979 and 1980. At the 1980 meeting, we decided that the first two summer schools had gone so well that they would now become an annual event. This was relevant to the second decision that we took: to see if we could issue the new Certificate in Religious Education (CRE) to successful participants.

The new CRE was announced by the Higher Education Council of the Bishops' Conference actually during our second summer school. It replaced the Catholic Teachers' Certificate (CTC), a qualification that in theory was required to teach in a Catholic school in England and Wales. The new certificate had a more developed syllabus and more stringent administrative procedures.

We looked at the new syllabus and compared it to what we were already delivering in our own programme. There was a pleasing interface! However, there was one important deficiency in our programme—the lack of a module relating to RE teaching in the classroom. Daniel and Teresa set to work remedying this. The four of us worked together on a new Life Light module entitled *Catechetics in the Classroom.* They provided the basic text (based on their own forthcoming book *Love and Meaning in Religious Education*) while we provided the distance-learning format. The new module was completed by late 1981.

Meanwhile I was approached by Father Patrick Purnell SJ, then Adviser to the Bishops on RE, to see whether it might be possible for CRE candidates who could not find a CRE course locally to obtain their certificate by a distance learning programme. We drew up a syllabus based on the CRE core curriculum and made a series of proposals. These were laid before the Bishops' Conference Board of Religious Studies in June 1981. Bishop Mullins, the then Chair of the Board, approved the syllabus and accepted most of the proposals. He authorized Life Light to award the Certificate of Religious Education, under the overall control of the Head of RS at Strawberry Hill.

It is fair to say that this way of working towards one's CRE proved to be successful. Some 250 teachers enrolled for our CRE course and by the time the CRE was terminated in the early 1990s, 204 participants in the programme had received their CRE certificates, while others were still completing their courses.

The Certificate in Adult Religious Education

The CRE, like its predecessor the CTC, was open to teachers only. Life Light was primarily concerned from the outset with the needs of adult RE. The Life Light Certificate continued to be used for a few years—mainly because the good folks who enrolled for it in the early days were more interested in the course itself than in acquiring a "bit of paper" at the end. With the passage of time, the need for a credible certificate increased. This was because successful course participants wanted to undertake some of the new parish ministry roles now available to the laity. In particular, they needed something to show to their parish priest that would help their applications.

There was much enthusiasm for adult RE in the 1980s. St Mary's set up their own Centre for Adult RE in 1984 under the inspirational leadership of Dr John Elias, author of *The Foundations and Practice of Adult Religious Education.* He and Sister Mary Boys headed our ninth summer school in 1986. So it seemed a good moment to approach Dr Michael Prior, the then Head of RS, with a proposal. Just as St Mary's awarded CREs to teachers through us, could they not extend this in respect of an almost identical course of study which would be accessible to non-teachers? Why "almost"? Daniel and Teresa's *Catechetics in the Classroom* module would be replaced by a new course relating to the adult setting of RE entitled *RE in the Parish.*

In 1984, John Elias, assisted by Sister Anne McDowell, ran a seven-week Saturday course on adult RE as part of the work of the new Centre of Adult RE. I found this course most stimulating. The Adult RE section of the course at Lumen Vitae was very solid and helpful, but it tended to emphasize the theory of adult RE at the expense of its practice. John was based in Chicago; academic circles in the United States had made enormous advances in the science of how adults learn, as well as related topics, and John now brought these ideas to the UK. My own module,

RE in the Parish, owes much to these sessions. I owe a debt of thanks to Anne McDowell who contributed many valuable insights to the final text.

Michael Prior agreed with my proposal for a Certificate of Adult RE. It finally started in 1987 and continued until the CRE was replaced by the Catholic Certificate in Religious Studies (CCRS) in 1992. (More about this in Chapter 9.)

Our debt to St Mary's

Life Light owes much to St Mary's. The date of my letter to Father Beirne was but a few months from when I was running Life Light from Room 18. Thanks to the RS department I was able to expand at a crucial time, even to delivering Certificate courses. Life Light fairly quickly became able again to deliver the level of service that we reached in the days of Hawkstone Hall Correspondence Courses. And it was thanks in particular to Daniel O'Leary that my own deep doubts about God were put to rest.

Contact with the RS department also empowered Heather and me to feel bold enough to explore new thinking—especially as regards Christian marriage—and I will describe these explorations in the next chapter.

8

Spirituality—from the Cloister to the Hearth

The theology of marriage

From the outset, the principal aim of my distance learning project was the religious education of adults. Since most adults spend most of their lives in a twosome relationship of marriage, a module on the theology of marriage just had to be included. It would also be a very fitting module to appear in a certificate course in adult RE.

I began planning this at Hawkstone. The first challenge had been to select a course book. None of those I considered said what I felt needed to be said in the post-Vatican II setting and amidst so much confusion following the publication of *Humanae Vitae* (1968). This encyclical, among other things, outlawed any act of sexual intercourse which was not open to the possibility of procreating a baby. Father Sean O'Riordan from the Redemptorist Irish province was giving a series of lectures at Hawkstone in 1975. I shared my problem with him, and he was instantly sympathetic. He revealed that he had just published a book on marriage which he thought might be of help. It was currently only available in Italian, but he hoped that Veritas Publications in Dublin would soon be publishing an English translation.

With the transfer from Hawkstone to Milton-under-Wychwood, this particular module made no further progress. For the moment, that is. But then Heather and I got married, settled into our little home and revelled in our new life together. On 4 March 1978, our village GP, Dr Scott, pronounced Heather pregnant. I'm not too sure of the cause-and-effect nexus here, but a few days later we were talking about the marriage module. I recounted the story so far, especially the problem of the course book. We were breakfasting at the time. At one point, our eyes met over the toast and marmalade as we simultaneously exclaimed: "Let's do it ourselves!"

Nearly all the Catholic books on marriage that I had considered had been written by priests. At that moment, it became obvious to both of us that the most appropriate authors of a new module on Christian marriage should be a Christian husband and wife. We would write it together: Heather concentrating on the sections she was most familiar with (the biblical ones), I on the subjects I knew more about (traditional marriage theology). The bits where we would share our marital spirituality . . . well, we would arrive at an agreed text together, somehow!

A journey of discovery

The exercise of writing this module was a journey of discovery. At the outset, we never realized that there was so much material in the Hebrew and Christian scriptures which could enrich the day-to-day lives of married people. We were already aware that being holy means being close to God. We were now to deepen our appreciation of just how close procreators are to their Creator: in a very real sense a husband and wife are continuing God's creative activity. Everything that leads up to procreation, from the first tentative exchange of glances, through fun together, courtship, engagement, marriage, setting up a home—it is *all* holy and smiled on by God, as indeed is all that follows. We eventually (and reluctantly) came to realize that the medieval theologians who thought that all this was somehow *un*holy, inferior to a life of celibacy, had simply got things wrong.

Why should we have thought this?

We traced this anti-sex line of thinking back to its origins. And they were *not* Christian origins! For the start of the story, we reached back to the Greek Orphic cults (sixth century BC). It was at this point that there appeared the first signs of *dualism* in Greek thinking. Various myths embodied the idea that we humans have a "dual" composition, that we are composed of two entirely separate and separable entities: a body and a soul. The body was believed to imprison the soul during life. After death, the soul was free to be rewarded or punished according to whether one had led a good life or a bad life.

During my course at Lumen Vitae, I had already learned that Pythagoras set up a religious community in Croton in southern Italy around 530 BC. This project was designed to enable its members to ensure a happy afterlife for themselves. The members had to observe celibacy—a practice motivated by the belief that sexual intercourse was bad for the soul. Plato (428–348 BC) taught that the body was inferior to the soul. Through the centuries which followed, his disciples tended to praise this spiritual part in us and at the same time played down the importance of the material body.

It goes without saying that in this climate of thought sexual intercourse got a fairly low rating! Sex was regarded as one of the least noble features of human life. Marriage was not highly valued. It, along with sexual intercourse, was esteemed primarily, and sometimes only, for its part in the continuation of human life. Thus, marriage was regarded at times as being merely a civic duty. A man who aspired to "higher" things, less material preoccupations, was well advised to have as little as possible to do with women, marriage and especially sexual intercourse. In the Roman Empire, celibacy became the fashion to such an extent that it threatened population levels. Emperor Augustus (27 BC–AD 14) passed a law in 18 BC which made marriage mandatory for all male Roman citizens.

Clearly from many points of view this Greek and, later, Roman outlook on marriage was at odds with that of the Jewish outlook. Dualism is almost entirely absent in Judaism. It would have been quite incompatible with the traditional theology underlying the accounts of creation in Genesis, not to mention the Song of Songs! It is incompatible too with the first proclamation of the gospel in Palestine.

We now speculated that if the Christian tradition on marriage had evolved directly from the earliest Jerusalem communities, and somehow bypassed certain aspects of Greek thinking, the theology of marriage would have had a very different history.

The writings on marriage by the Fathers of the Church (the more important Christian literature up to the time of St Bernard of Clairvaux

(1090–1153)), almost all of whom had received a Greek-orientated education, very definitely followed the Greek line rather than that of the Jewish tradition.[1] Why they should have taken this line is explained by the history of the first and second centuries AD. Rome was at war with the Jews from AD 66, culminating in the horrendous capture of Jerusalem by Titus, the burning of the Temple (AD 70) and the Siege of Masada (AD 73). Simon ben Goria was brought to Rome to feature in a Triumph and was executed in the summer of AD 71 amid popular Roman hatred of the Jews. Anti-Semitic feeling remained strong for centuries, in fact until recently, having been fed by successive generations of Christians who (quite wrongly) accused the Jews of deicide. Not unnaturally many of the early "intellectual" Gentile converts to Christianity would have felt not a little uncomfortable with the fact that Jesus had belonged to a nation with which Rome was then at war. Thus, there was a tendency in early Christian writing to play down Jewish connections and emphasize all and everything in Greek and Roman thinking that could be "baptized" into the new faith.

In this way, a whole package of concepts, ideas, attitudes, assumptions, values and beliefs came to be imported from the Greek and Roman world into the infant Church. With the passage of time these attitudes have come to be identified with the Christian Church itself. This is a major cause of why many young people today regard Christianity as not "cool".

With regard to marriage, these imports meant that early Christian writers and thinkers had to deal with the sexual hang-ups of the followers of Pythagoras, Plato and others. They had to find answers to questions which neither Jesus nor the Jews had ever raised. Sexual pleasure, human loving, marriage and intercourse had been prized as God's gifts. They required no further justification. Now all of these gifts were being regarded as degrading.

Anti-marriage sentiments are commonplace from the early second century AD; for example, in the *Pastor of Hermas* (c. AD 130), and in the writings of Justin Martyr (c.100–65), Tatian (c.110–72)—who, according to Clement of Alexandria, was the first to suggest that Jesus never married—and Origen (c.185–254), whose extreme views on asceticism led him to castrate himself. In most of these writings, celibacy was recommended where possible. Marriage was tolerated as a remedy for sexual desire, and the main justification of intercourse was the procreation of children. All other sexual activity was mere gratification, self-indulgence, giving way to the weakness of the flesh. It was certainly prejudicial to the spiritual life and endangered one's chances of salvation.

Some of this passed into the monasteries of the Middle Ages. Elements of this way of thinking about the spiritual life featured on a regular basis in the lectures and conferences in my noviciate and at Hawkstone. Crucially, it also entered into the medieval treatises on marriage (which were almost always developed by monks and friars). During the centuries before the discoveries of modern gynaecology, the role of the female in reproduction was underestimated. It was thought that the male semen was simply implanted in the female, as seed in a plant pot, and thus grew into a new human life. These perceived natural processes of reproduction were thought to imply moral norms of sexual behaviour. The fate of the male seed was seen to be crucially important: to frustrate its purpose, for example in masturbation, was compared to abortion.

A major concern in these treatises was to establish the criteria for a legally valid marriage. This was very useful as women all too commonly suffered from forced marriage. The Church began to insist on the presence of a priest and two witnesses for a marriage to be recognized as valid. This greatly promoted human happiness.

But over time the legal aspect of marriage unfortunately became more important than any other aspect. Marriage came to be regarded in the first place as a contract, with rights and duties on both sides. Marriage problems were analysed from a contractual point of view—rather than a psychological, emotional and loving one. Right up to the late twentieth century, marriage preparation consisted largely in fulfilling the requirements of Canon Law.

The Second Vatican Council

Heather and I found it a refreshing experience to revisit the contribution of the Second Vatican Council. *Lumen gentium*, the Council's *Constitution on the Church,* set out to restore the biblical perspective of marriage, and this enabled a fresh spirituality of married life to be sketched out.

> All the faithful of Christ, of whatever rank or status, are called to the fullness of the Christian life and to the perfection of charity ... Married couples and Christian parents should follow their own proper path to holiness by faithful love, sustaining one another in grace throughout the entire length of their lives. They should imbue their offspring, lovingly welcomed from God, with Christian truths and evangelical virtues.[2]
>
> Authentic married love is caught up into divine love ... Such love, merging the human with the divine, leads the spouses to a free and mutual gift of themselves, a gift proving itself by gentle affection and by deed. Such love pervades the whole of their lives ... This love is uniquely expressed and perfected through the marital act. The actions within marriage by which a couple are united intimately and chastely are noble and worthy ones. Expressed in a manner which is truly human, these actions signify and promote that mutual self-giving by which spouses enrich each other with a joyful and thankful will.[3]

The Second Vatican Council declared that it was the will of Christ that *all* his followers were called to holiness and to the fullness of the Christian life. It had previously been widely imagined that only clergy and religious (through the pursuit of the three "evangelical counsels" of poverty, chastity and obedience) were called to the fullness of the Christian life. Now the Council called for a radical change of perspective. We were to view as appropriate settings for holiness of life not only the Sisters' chapel but also the parish church, not only the monk's cell but also the three-bedroom semi, not only the monastic community but the village/neighbourhood community—not only the cloister but also the hearth.

Married spirituality: some old paths

This was quite a revolutionary change. It had indeed long been thought that the fullness of the Christian life was mainly the exclusive preserve of religious and clergy. However, in the Catholic Church, the married and the marriageable account for some 95 per cent of Catholics throughout the world. Hence it can only be regarded as a sad fact that throughout the Christian centuries the vast majority of writings on the subject of "spirituality" had come from priests and religious, and were addressed mainly to other priests and religious. The central concerns of the conferences of St Bernard of Clairvaux, St Ignatius Loyola, St Teresa of Avila, St John of the Cross, St Francis de Sales and others are the problems and opportunities facing the *individual* soul on his/her path to perfection. The envisaged context is for the most part celibate and/or monastic, with an understandable emphasis upon the needs for good order in the community, the avoidance of distractions and sexual sin. This context has contributed certain features to spiritual writing: the emphasis upon *private* prayer, withdrawal into periodic solitude, personal asceticism, silence, strengthening of the will, low self-esteem, obedience to directors, suspicion of the opposite sex, a certain "churchiness" and so on. The characteristic setting for such writing is "God—me—my neighbour".

Furthermore, there was the pessimistic attitudes of some Church figures to sex and marriage. Spiritual writing often gave the impression that if one really wanted to be holy, one would have as little as possible to do with either sex or marriage! This impression can only have been reinforced by the fact that there are so very few married saints—and even they have been canonized for *other* reasons, like martyrdom (for example, St Thomas More) or because they took a vow of celibacy (like St Henry VI)!

For all these reasons, the "old paths" to lay holiness were largely adaptations of monastic and convent spirituality. The fruits of contemplation and the spiritual experience of the monastery were shared with the wider Christian community through spiritual books and manuals designed for religious, through spiritual retreats held in religious houses, and through parish missions directed by religious. The "Third Orders" of certain religious Orders were an extension of the same idea, with the laity sharing an Order's spiritual heritage and (as far as the non-celibate state allowed) taking part in the spiritual exercises of the Order, often with elaborate probation and initiation procedures involving a period of noviciate and profession. This path is often a real help for the unattached lay person who is better situated to observe silence, solitude, private prayer and the recommended mortifications and who can more easily get away for days in the monastery.

A path of our own? A theological structure

The path of religious life is trodden by *individuals* who have consecrated their communitarian lives to God through the public profession of the vows of poverty, chastity and obedience. As such, religious-life spirituality can have only limited application to those of us who live a two-in-one-flesh existence. A special kind of family might find it stimulating to make mini-monasteries of their homes, with reading at table and periods of silence to cultivate an atmosphere of prayer and recollection, but most of us would find such a project impractical for a whole variety of reasons. That is why the Council refers to a path that is "proper" (or "appropriate") to married couples. But is there such a path?

To establish a path, and following the lead given by the Second Vatican Council, we had only to refer back to the authors of Genesis. There we see that we are like God precisely in our maleness-*and*-femaleness (Genesis 5:1–2). Husband and wife are thus immediately "caught up into the divine", close to God (and hence "holy") by virtue of their state.

A vivid illustration of the Hebrew ideal of rejoicing in the man-woman relationship under God's smile is found in the five songs of the Song of Songs. These love songs progress from love's awakening (1:2) to final consummation (7:12), via the normal and natural joys and uncertainties of courtship. Like all love songs, these songs search around the contemporary world for ways of vividly expressing the lovers' admiration for each other. Hence some of the imagery used is lost on us, while other sentiments are universal and span the centuries; for example, "I am sick with love" (2:5); "On my bed at night I sought the man who is my sweetheart" (3:1); "I caught him, would not let him go" (3:4). He tells her: "You ravish my heart with a single one of your glances" (4:9). She promises him: "I shall give you the gift of my love" (7:12).

The Song of Songs is a celebration of love and faithfulness between a man and a woman; there is nothing startling, shocking or crude in it. Effusions of loving sentiments between boys and girls are characteristic of every epoch—our own day included. What then *is* significant in the Song of Songs? First, these ancient love songs mention God only once: "Love . . . is the flame of God himself" (8:6). (Human love is thus caught up into divine love.)

Second, these songs are nevertheless actually in the Bible!

Heather and I talked much about these two features of the Song of Songs. One evening we were watching television, as Johnny Mathis was singing "When I fall in love, it will be forever—or I'll never fall in love . . . .", a popular song which was written in the 1950s and recorded many times by many artists. Heather observed: "If *that* song had been around in Palestine at the time, it would have got into the Song of Songs!"

We began to wonder whether we should not look again at our modern love songs—see them with new eyes and sing them with new heart—by appreciating them within that overall faith-context intended in Genesis. Then we could perhaps bring ourselves to a further perception: that we love, honour, praise and indeed worship God quite simply by celebrating and rejoicing in the gift of our relationship as a loving couple. When we express our love for each other, we *thereby* worship God. "Close to nature, close to God", we rejoice in God's smile.

The central importance of marriage to Christian living is a claim that is based not only on the Old Testament, but also on the New. Even in theological circles, it is sometimes still presumed that Jesus had little positive to say about human love and marriage.[4] But in fact, the sayings and example of Jesus contain a wealth of inspiration, support, encouragement and guidance in the concrete details of married life. At one point in our research, we took a number of the sayings of Jesus. We then imagined that the two of us were in the crowd listening to Jesus preaching and applying his words to our own married setting. There was a huge amount of relevance!

> "I give you a new commandment: love one another. Just as I have loved you, you also must love one another."
>
> *John 13:34*

"A man can have no greater love than to lay down his life for his friends."

John 15:13

"You must love your neighbour as yourself."

Matthew 22:39

"Always treat others as you would like them to treat you."

Matthew 7:12

"Give, and there will be gifts for you: a full measure, pressed down, shaken together and running over will be poured into your lap. Because the amount you measure out is the amount you will be given back."

Luke 6:38

"Do not judge, and you will not be judged: because the judgements you will give are the judgements you will get, and the amount you measure out is the amount you will be given."

Matthew 7:1–2

"Do good and lend without any hope of return. Be compassionate as your Father is compassionate. Do not condemn and you will not be condemned yourselves. Grant pardon and you will be pardoned.

Luke 6:35–7

"If (your brother) wrongs you seven times a day, and seven times a day comes back to you and says, 'I am sorry!', you must forgive him."

Luke 17:3–4

"So then, if you are bringing your offering to the altar and there remember that your brother has something against you, leave

> your offering there before the altar, go and be reconciled with your brother first, and then come back and present your offering."
>
> *Matthew 5:23–4*

All of us do well to take to heart what Jesus is saying here. But, in the order of priority, these points apply to married people most of all. They have indeed "laid down their lives" for one another. We *need* to be sharing, generous with our time, thoughtful in our presents, non-judgemental and forgiving. Reconciliation is more important than going to church!

Tension between a husband and wife—and the need to resolve it—is perhaps rather more urgent than tension between two monks! (Although both situations call for generosity of spirit.)

When we

- show to each other something of Jesus' love for us
- treat each other as we would like to be treated ourselves
- give to each other and receive in return
- are reconciled after a bout of selfishness
- make love

we know that these are holy times. We know that Jesus is present to us as he promised. When we *pro*create, we unite ourselves to the *Creator*, the God of Life. If holiness means being close to God, then it's just got to be one of the holiest things we ever do! Our new son/daughter may in their turn procreate their own sons/daughters. The dimensions of our procreating are thus far-reaching. They spread beyond the confines of our home and the life-span of our years and have an eternal dimension.

Vatican II re-emphasized the biblical dimensions of marriage which it saw as a relationship founded on love between two people. The loving couple live out a relationship that is vital for the future of humanity, "caught up into the divine", close to God in its love and fruitfulness—a relationship that is *holy in itself.* All this was in stark contrast to the concept of marriage being primarily a contract.

Some Christian specifics

We then spent a lot of time thinking about the specifically Christian enrichment of the husband-wife relationship.

Relationship is at the base of the essential Christian message. Jesus' message centred upon the concept of the kingdom of God.[5] A kingdom is a collection of persons under the rule of a "king". Two sets of relationships are involved:

1. the relationship between the "king" and the community, and
2. the relationship between each member of that community and each *other* member of that community.

Corresponding to these two sets of relationship are the Two Great Commandments. Jesus himself summarized the heart of his message in Matthew 22:37–40, where he prioritizes our need to love God and to love our neighbour.

When a group of people enter into these new relationships with God and with one another, the kingdom of God appears among them. This kind of community was first set up at Pentecost. Acts 1–2 describes the transformation of a small group of Jesus' followers who were very unsure of themselves into a true community which "lived together and owned everything in common". In the Upper Room in which the disciples had *come together*, in view of everything that had happened to them during the preceding weeks it was a time for putting one's cards on the table, preferably facing up, and for the truth of the one to be exposed to the truth of the other, a time for complete frankness and continuous prayer (Acts 1:14).[6]

These were the circumstances in which the Holy Spirit appeared and in which he was felt to be remaining.

Our own coming together

We then interfaced these points with our own love story. When we fell in love and eventually decided to give ourselves to each other in a permanent union of our two personalities, it was in many ways a setting which bore comparison to the first Pentecost. We too did not know what the future would bring: fulfilment and happiness, or frustration and misery. If we had quizzed each other at that point (which we didn't!), we would certainly as Christians have expressed our intention of aiming selflessly to love each other "as I have loved you" in accordance with Jesus' higher standard.

We speculated that in every such loving relationship there comes a moment of deep confrontation, when the truth of the one is exposed to the truth of the other—an "I and thou" moment—when there is no longer any need to play-act in the presence of the other, pretending to be better than one is, trying to impress, cutting a good image. All that belongs to an earlier stage of the relationship. This is a moment when both can accept each other for what they are—no more, no less. It is a moment of truth, when one's cards are on the table and facing up. It is in these circumstances that the Holy Spirit comes to two such people and is commonly experienced as remaining. Two people have *come together* to share a life of love in faith, to live it out together in the closest-knit of all communities: marriage.

Just as it is the Holy Spirit that is the bond of unity within the Christian community, supports it and builds it up, so it is the Holy Spirit, we thought, that is the bond of unity between the husband and wife, that supports this new infant community, and builds it up into a dynamic as well as a loving interpersonal relationship, "the domestic Church"—as St John Paul II called it.[7] The parallels between the coming together of the Christian community and that of the Christian couple in marriage are such that it is likely that the same spiritual structures obtain. It is here, we believed, that we should locate that "something special" which Christian tradition has always felt was present when two Christians come together in marriage. A dynamic appears over and above the natural interaction of human love. St Clement, writing about AD 150, asks: "Who are the two or three gathered together in the name of Christ, in whose midst is the

Lord? Are they not man, wife and child, because man and wife are joined by God?" The third-century theologian Tertullian sees this moment of coming together as the beginning of a new religious order[8]—a relevant insight in this context! The community of the Church, the community of religious, and the Christian marriage community all have this in common: the Holy Spirit is experienced as indwelling all three. The twentieth-century Dominican theologian Edward Schillebeeckx puts it this way: "Where two people have found each other in true love, God is already in their midst."[9]

We concluded that a path to married holiness and to the fullness of the Christian life certainly exists. We discerned the basis of a spirituality which would reach all aspects of the male-female relationship, not just to the actually married, but the marriageable and (since love is stronger than death) those who have been married in the past. We were excited at the prospect of constructing a spirituality that sat just as comfortably upon the two-in-one mode of living of the married, as traditional spirituality sat meaningfully upon monastic and convent life. The monastery has fittings, decorations, statues and architecture designed to promote an awareness of the presence of God. The home is full of God-given life and love—in every room, outside in the street and beyond—all calling for a loving response. The hearth *can* be as holy as the cloister, and the estate semi as sacred a place as the convent, for in both there could be a comparable prayerful openness to the Father, a sincere following of the Son, and an awareness of the Holy Spirit indwelling married love in all its dimensions.

The prayer of the loving couple

The next step was to take elements of the spiritual life—especially prayer and liturgy—and view them from our own married standpoint.

Before she was married, Heather—good Catholic girl that she was—prayed often (she told me). She would go to her room, read a Bible passage and pray about it. Then she married me, and this practice stopped. Marriage had torpedoed our prayer lives! We felt bad about this.

For a short time, as I have said, we would spread out the *Prayer of the Church* on our laps and pray Compline together. This helped.

The experience of writing our *Theology of Marriage* module changed a number of our attitudes—prayer among them. Prayer can take many forms: the common element is an openness to God, "a raising of the heart and mind" as the Penny Catechism described it. We had come to appreciate our little home as a place of much love, life and laughter where it was natural to give God a grateful nod every now and then. We decided that, on reflection, we were in fact praying quite a lot—when the mood took us rather than in accordance with pre-set timetables. We would enjoy a quiet moment holding hands in the presence of God, inspired in a hundred different ways: need, emotion, music, an anniversary, after a romantic meal, a meaningful section of a film, a success, a failure, a piece of nostalgia, making love—especially making love! By sharing these moments with God, whether actual words are spoken or not, we came to realize that we were actually praying. We were raising up our hearts and minds to God. Like millions of couples the world over, last thing at night we would cuddle up and tell each other "I love you." And, in our case, this became our Compline!

Many couples and parents do not recognize such moments as prayer—because they are not on their knees verbalizing in separate rooms or using official prayers. And so they feel guilty, because the opportunities for such prayer arise less and less often as the years go by and as the family grows up. This sense of guilt often eats away at their spiritual lives. It would be a great service to family prayer if this sense of guilt could be removed.

When as loving couples we put ourselves in the presence of God in prayer, strictly speaking there seems little need (unless some find the practice helpful) either to be or to imagine ourselves as being within some sacred place, like a church or shrine. *Our setting is in itself holy.* Our togetherness is in itself a sacred setting, within which openness to God in prayer, the raising of our hearts and minds to God, is altogether natural. The Holy Spirit is present to us in our loving relationship. Actual praying may take many forms: verbalizing, silence, contemplation, petition, praise, adoration and thanksgiving for so many good things. We can pray a Psalm, a hymn, a scripture passage, a family event, a quarrel, a good experience. We can pray regularly or as the mood takes us. No two couples pray alike.

The opening chapters of the Bible affirm God as the God of Life, as the Creator and Sustainer of all life, and imaged in terms of our male-female unity. Sex and life are so intimately connected that the one is the condition of the continuity of the other. Making love is therefore necessarily intimately connected with the God of Life—as procreators to their Creator—and hence rightly belongs to the sphere of the sacred. A concern of the writers of these early chapters of Genesis was to transfer sexuality "from the sphere of the fertility cults . . . into the sphere of the worship of God"[10]—its rightful setting.

Making love is a liturgy in which the loving couple worship God. It is a holy time of closeness to God, Creator and Sustainer of life, as we sustain our life of love and even, on occasions, *pro*create life. It has its own ritual, different for each couple, ever changing with the passage of time, yet with a constant feature of joyful playfulness, mutual stimulation and deep communion of minds and bodies. This is a liturgy with a climax point, with ecstasy bordering on mystic union with transcendent reality, followed by a period of peace, rest and thanksgiving to God for the gift of sexual pleasure and to each other for mediating that gift. No other liturgy praises God like this liturgy, nor serves so essentially the eternal purposes of the Creator.

Praying with our children

With guilt replaced by the joy and fulfilment of praying naturally and authentically, we should be able better to involve our children in our prayer. The prayer of the loving couple may evolve naturally into family prayer. When we as parents face the "problem" of teaching our children how to pray, many of us find ourselves in the position of a swimming instructor who cannot swim, or perhaps does not swim! Prayer, like swimming, calls for faith. We can "go through the motions" of praying with our children, tell them what to do, whom and what to pray for and so on. But if we ourselves as their parents do not have that spirit of prayer within us, we cannot hope to communicate it to our children. We feel that most of the problems we parents raise about "how to teach our children to pray" would be the easier to resolve if we ourselves prayed authentically and honestly. As parents we pass on so many things: language, values, faith, genes, brown eyes . . . How our children talk to other people is to a great extent determined by us as parents. Yet when it comes to how our children talk to God, we all too often are content to "leave it to the RE teacher", reach for the nearest book of prayers for children or search for an appropriate app. We should try to see how we may involve our children in our praying, and so pass on our prayerful attitudes naturally.

Husbands and wives, and even whole families, have been praying set prayers together for centuries—although this practice has been in decline of late. Nowadays family prayer seems to be going in the direction of less formal praying, less prolonged, and (especially where small children are involved) centred on food and sleep: home-made prayers at table and at bedtime.

Liturgy

We noticed that we began to value the liturgy differently in the light of our ongoing research. Around the house we hummed the tunes we had sung at church. The Bidding Prayers often served as a model for our intercessions. Heather and I routinely snuggled up after Communion and felt very close to both Christ and one another in this sacred moment. The Sign of Peace between us became qualitatively different from that exchanged with other fellow parishioners. On occasions, the Penitential Rite at the beginning of Mass was a quite richer experience, especially when the whole family took part in it together!

We concluded that the liturgy is indeed a support of married couples and their families.

The sacramentality of marriage

In the light of our research, we could more easily discern the sacramentality of marriage. This had been a problem in the Middle Ages: some theologians just could not see how marriage with its lovemaking could have anything to do with the other sacraments. Some recommended considering the consecration of a bishop to be a separate sacrament from the sacrament of order, to make up the number of the sacraments to seven (seen as a priority at the time). Nowadays we can locate the sacramentality of marriage precisely where it has been looked for over the centuries, namely in the loving *relationship* between husband and wife which has been "caught up into divine love".[11] It is precisely in that relationship, where Jesus himself declared that he would be, that we find a great sacrament of God's love, comparable to any of the other sacraments, but where the ministers are not priests, deacons or other representatives of the hierarchy but rather (according to the constant tradition of the Church in the West) the partners themselves.

The being and wellbeing of the human race

Our research focused on the spirituality and fulfilments of marriage. We became aware that we humans experience a sense of fulfilment when we do anything that promotes the actual being of the human race. The prime example, of course, is procreating new life. But this sense of fulfilment is experienced also by persons *other* than parents. I know a former midwife, now retired, who has been at the birth of almost all the younger inhabitants of her neighbourhood. A more quietly fulfilled person you will not meet! This is because another well-attested source of fulfilment is promoting the *wellbeing* of human life. Included here is a vast and disparate multitude of selfless individuals who devote their lives to the many forms of public service—doctors, health carers, teachers and other professional service providers to mention just a few, and, of course, not omitting to include the Sisters, priests and religious too.

We easily relate procreation to Creation and see how God must smile on procreators. We must also be aware of how close to God are all those who, in whatever form, contribute to the ongoing process of life and its evolution, from the midwife to the space scientist.

Time to share our findings

Heather and I were very excited about our *Theology of Marriage* module which we completed in June 1978. We offered it to course participants of the Certificate in Adult Religious Education (CARE) as an optional subject. In the next chapter, I will share the reactions to our new module.

9

Helping Out All Round

From the start of Hawkstone Hall Correspondence Courses in 1974, I was surprised by the interest from far and wide that became evident. Priests, religious and laity, both in these isles and as far away as New Zealand, perceived an interface between their current needs and what we could offer. Quite understandably, this interest faded with my laicization. At times, I wondered darkly whether it would ever surface again. It did—and in unexpected ways.

Working with the Church of England

Heather and I completed *The Theology of Marriage* on 5 June 1978. In the following days, we printed and dispatched the first copies as part of the CARE course. One of these copies landed on the desk of the Bishop of Lichfield, Kenneth Skelton. As Bishop of Matabeleland in Zimbabwe from 1962 to 1970, he became famous for publicly opposing Ian Smith's declaration of independence from the UK in 1966. He was appointed Bishop of Lichfield in 1975 and headed the Church of England Marriage Commission for a number of years. In 1978, his commission produced the *Lichfield Report on Marriage and the Church's Task.*

On 30 June 1978, Heather and I received a visit from Prebendary Ian Calvert. He had been sent by the bishop. Ian told us that the bishop was impressed by our text and wondered if an Anglican version could be considered. The idea was that it might serve as background reading for those who would be considering the *Lichfield Report* in the weeks and months ahead.

Ian showed clear-eyed understanding of our initial reaction. The Church of England looking for inspiration from the Catholic Church—in matters of marriage, for heaven's sake! Ian explained that, at that point at least, there was not too much serious literature on Christian marriage and that Bishop Kenneth had been attracted by the idea of a Christian husband and wife sharing their first-hand experience of Christian marriage.

I put it to Ian that the C of E had had married clergy for four centuries and that one could have expected at least some of the more articulate clergy couples to have reflected on their experience in the light of the gospel, shared their thoughts with their parishioners and thus enriched Christian marriage. Apparently, this had not happened to any large extent.

We came across this same reticence within the Catholic context as well. In April 1980 we ran a Life Light stall at the Clifton diocese Vocations Exhibition. There we met Ian and Teresa MacCallum, who were active members of Marriage Encounter. We talked about this reticence. It seems that couples do not parade their married bliss, and this for a number of reasons. Chief among these is that those who *do* quite often are perceived as covering up unhappiness! There is also the kindly motive of not wanting to bring discomfort to the unmarried. Teresa invited Heather and me to contribute an article on this reticence to *Encounter Spirit*—the periodical of Clifton Marriage Encounter. Our article appeared the following month. Entitled "Join us in writing about marriage", it invited the members of Marriage Encounter to write in with snippets of married experience. Forty years on, we still await the first snippet!

Heather and I enjoyed a series of most pleasant and constructive working sessions with Ian Calvert and his wife Mary, both in our home and also in their Forton Rectory in Newport, Shropshire, where Ian was parish priest. Mary was a member of the General Synod and shared with us something of how the Synod actually works. We became quite close; Ian and Mary let us use their Welsh cottage in Trevor for our very first family holiday in 1979.

The result was *Marriage Today*—a resource pack for small groups. It comprised handout booklets for the participants and more detailed notes for the group leader. We went to print in February 1979. The take-up exceeded our expectations. Throughout this period of working with Ian and Mary, we were pleasantly surprised at how easy it had been for us, as Catholics, to work so smoothly and productively with the Church of England.

Habemus Babam!

Meanwhile, Philip Andrew Harris was born in the John Radcliffe Hospital in Oxford on 25 October 1978. In those days, husbands were beginning to be required to dress up and be present at the moment of birth. My very first fleeting thought was "Poor chap! You've got me for your dad!" This quickly gave way to a transcendental experience—for both of us, I'm sure.

Heather's family was ecstatic. Sadly, Heather's dad, Harry Farr, had died in February. He would have been as delighted, as Noreen manifestly was, to be living through the beginning of this next chapter in the story of our family. My Mum was thrilled too; I discerned that I was now being viewed in a somewhat more positive light!

It was Heather herself who designed the card which announced Philip's safe arrival. That year, 1978, was the year of the three popes. Paul VI died on 6 August; John Paul I was elected on the 26th but died on 28 September. John Paul II was elected on 16 October—a week before Philip was born. After each papal election, the traditional white smoke appeared over the Vatican and a senior prelate announced "*Habemus papam*—we have a Pope". It was unusual for this to happen twice in two months. "*Habemus papam*" became common parlance for a brief period. So my ever-inventive wife drew a picture comprising the Vatican chimney issuing white smoke together with a suitably vested bishop proclaiming Urbi et Orbi, to the city and the world: "*habemus babam*". Our clerical friends loved it!

Maryvale

In English Catholic history, Old Oscott to the north west of Birmingham is special, a place of pilgrimage dating back to the Middle Ages. Here will be found England's oldest chapel dedicated to the Sacred Heart. Oscott Seminary was founded here in 1794. St John Henry Newman (1801–90) briefly lived here from 1846 and renamed the site Maryvale. The Sisters of Mercy ran an orphanage in Maryvale House between 1851 and 1980. In 1980, Archbishop Dwyer made use of the vacated house for the establishment of the Adult Centre for Catechetics and appointed a young priest to run it.

Sadly, this first director of the Centre died suddenly—apparently as a result of excessive anxiety over the project he had been commissioned to organize. Shortly after this tragedy I contacted Father (later Canon) Daniel McHugh, who had just been appointed as the new director. He shared some of the immediate problems he faced. He needed to set up courses for adults, but he lacked the resources to do this.

I proposed a way out of his problem. By 1980, I had a respectable number of Life Light modules which I would put at his disposal. Life Light could offer home tuition in any one module to as many adults in the large archdiocese of Birmingham as would be interested, and this could be followed up by get-togethers at Maryvale. We agreed to run a pilot scheme.

The first module we used was *Liturgy*. One hundred and fifty people enrolled. At the get-together there was an unexpectedly high degree of enthusiasm from the participants. Father McHugh wanted more, so together we set up a two-year Certificate course in adult RE along the same lines. He was so happy with the result that he wrote a very positive write-up.[1] By the time he was writing we had attracted over 400 enrolments.

The Maryvale Adult Centre for Catechetics was now very definitely in business! Soon speakers became available from the nearby seminary at Oscott College and Life Light could turn to other deserving causes. The Centre was renamed the Maryvale Institute. It has developed enormously since then, offering part-time and distance learning theological degree courses, and other catechetical qualifications validated by the Open

University, Liverpool Hope University and the Notre Dame Faculty in Paris.

Nigeria

An early member of staff at Maryvale was the Marist Brother Fillan. He recommended Life Light to his confreres in Nigeria who were experiencing difficulties in organizing the ongoing tuition of their junior members in the aftermath of the Biafran Civil War (1967–70). In June 1980 we tailor-made a course of study for each one of the young Marist students as part of their noviciate and post-noviciate studies. Some very interesting essays arrived. Many contained deep first-hand reflections stimulated by harrowing episodes during the years of conflict in which their writers had been involved.

"Living Liturgy"

Reports of the Maryvale liturgy course spread around the dioceses. Father (later Monsignor) Anthony Boylan, the then National Adviser for Liturgical Formation, contacted me to see if a similar short course in liturgy could be organized in London. The result was a seven-week period of home study using the text of our module on the Liturgy, interfacing with a Friday-to-Sunday residential at Maria Assumpta College in Kensington in September 1981.

The short prospectus somewhat enthusiastically stated that

> Here is a NEW approach to liturgical formation: a short period of home study linked with a pleasant and profitable weekend get-together. First you take part in a correspondence course of seven programmed lectures in the comfort of your home. Then you will be welcomed to Maria Assumpta College in Kensington for a residential weekend. Here you will be able to meet your fellow participants and take part in meaningful liturgy.

The weekend session was led by Father Boylan himself. He was aided by Father John Glen (who was for a time a curate to my brother Tony in the Northampton diocese) and also by Sister Patricia England OP.

It was an unusually hot weekend which greatly disrupted sleep by night and required much liquid refreshment by day! The inputs from Fathers Boylan and Glen were very helpful and stimulating. Sister Patricia provided a lot of thought-provoking material, although it was her misfortune to have been allocated the hot Saturday afternoon. At one unforgettable point, faced with a number of drooping participants, she suddenly broke joyously into the three-fold "Alleluia!" chant of the Easter Vigil. She immediately regained our attention!

The Diocese of Wrexham

Father (later Canon) Paddy Breen was one of the most inspirational priests with whom I have worked. Enthused by his course at Corpus Christi in London, and in his capacity as Religious Adviser to the diocese of Menevia, he was ever trying to find new ways of blowing the spirit of Vatican II throughout the length and breadth of his diocese.

He organized a twelve-session Ministry for Lay People course in Bangor in 1982 and kindly invited me to run the two opening sessions on "The Role of the Parish Priest" and "Tomorrow's Laity". During the years that followed, Paddy and I worked on a number of events. In the process of arranging these he regularly shared with me his problem of providing for the new diocese of Wrexham (in which he later found himself). This had been set up in 1987, having previously been part of the diocese of Menevia. The new diocese of Wrexham had a minuscule Catholic population scattered over a wide area, stretching from Gwynedd in the west to Flintshire in the east and involving many rather slow journeys between parishes. The division of the dioceses had also apparently left Wrexham worse off financially. Resources for RE were stretched. The diocesan CRE course, based in Cartrefle College in Wrexham, was being run on a shoestring by one of the Catholic lecturers, Mr Bernard Parkinson. When he retired from the college in 1989 there was a danger that the diocese would have no CRE course at all. Paddy contacted me again.

At that time, as we have seen, Life Light was running a nationwide CRE course in conjunction with St Mary's, Strawberry Hill, which oversaw the issue of certificates. I proposed to Paddy that we might tweak this arrangement. Using the approved distance learning CRE course materials, we could set up a Wrexham diocese CRE course, with a residential component somewhere within the diocese. With his customary enthusiasm, Paddy entered into negotiations with the Loreto Sisters in Llandudno. As a result, the Life Light Wrexham CRE (and the later CCRS) course held annual residential sessions at the Loreto Centre for some twenty years. Teachers and trainee teachers worked from home through their two-year courses in any part of the diocese and came together to Llandudno once a year to share their experiences, problems and insights.

The programme was self-financing; it did not cost the diocesan authorities a single penny. There was also a benefit to Life Light: we could now issue CRE certificates in the name of the diocese (without having to bother St Mary's). Of much greater benefit was being able to work with Sister Bernadette Foley, a Brigidine Sister from Denbigh. A teacher trainer herself, Bernadette contributed magnificently to the success of the Llandudno sessions. She was also an authority on the "Here I Am" RE programme for primary schools and helped in the production of the Life Light module *RE in the Primary School.* Sadly, both Canon Paddy and Sister Bernadette are no longer with us, but the fruits of their collaboration remain. Life Light will always be indebted to them for their untiring labours in difficult circumstances.

It was around this time (1989) that we changed our name from "Life Light Correspondence Courses" to "Life Light Home Study Courses". The reason for this change? The popular sitcom *Last of the Summer Wine* (at that time the longest running sitcom in the world), as well as other TV shows, were frequently making jokes about correspondence courses. So we thought it was time for a change.

And other dioceses/institutes . . .

I enjoyed a number of productive and stimulating sessions with Debbie Jones with a view to setting up a CRE course for the diocese of East Anglia. I remember well the get-together of the course participants at Our Lady's in Stowmarket in November 1988. Halfway through the first segment of the all-day session, a middle-aged man sauntered in and took a seat in the back row. He seemed moderately engaged with the proceedings. At coffee break, he made his way over to me.

"You don't know who I am," he told me.

"I think you're about to tell me," I ventured.

"I'm Alan Clarke!"

I thanked the bishop most profusely for not putting me off my delivery of the first section of the day (as he would have done if he had arrived in his purple ecclesiastical garb!). We became friends immediately and he gave much encouragement to the work.

We were also able to help out in other dioceses by stepping in at short notice to deliver a module where the original resource provider had become suddenly unavailable. For example, between April and June 1988 Life Light provided a module on Christology in Brentwood Cathedral for thirty-five participants.

Heather and I also worked with the Housetop Centre for a while. Under the directorship of John Wijngaards, Housetop pioneered the use of video catechetics in Catholic England, producing among many other titles *The Seven Circles of Prayer* and *Walking on Water.* In May 1988, John invited us to write a booklet entitled *Parents Praying* to accompany the video *Prayer in your Home.*

Plater College

Life Light was approached in 1991 by Plater College, Oxford. Founded in 1922 by Father Leo O'Hea SJ in memory of Father Charles Plater SJ (1878–1921), Plater College offered generations of students with connections to Trade Unions the possibility of a university-standard education in circumstances where it would have been otherwise unavailable. The curriculum incorporated generous provision for the study of Catholic Social Teaching (CST)—befitting a college which once bore the title "Catholic Workers' College".

In the early 1990s, a modification was being made to the structure of the Plater course. The two-year introductory course of study was being replaced by a one-year course. To facilitate this change, the suggestion was made to us that we might be able to offer potential students a short distance-learning course prior to their coming up to Oxford. It was agreed that a module on the basics of Christian belief would be an appropriate subject area. A programme was set up, comprising home study with the services of a postal tutor, three supervised essays and a confidential report for the college on each course participant.

The programme began in February 1992. With the ongoing support of the Principal Michael Blades, between 1992 and shortly before the closure of the college in 2005, some 300 students worked through this programme. Many worked from overseas, especially Malta (where Charles Plater was held in high esteem), and it was an enlightening experience to tutor such a diverse group of students.

In May 1995, I attended a number of highly informative meetings at Plater at which members of the teaching staff explored the possibility of producing a distance-learning course on Catholic Social Teaching, integrated with a short residential period at the college during vacation periods. Although this particular project never became a reality, the experience of planning its details aroused a new interest in me. I had long looked for ways of highlighting the relevance of the Catholic Church to the actual details of modern life. The Plater meetings enthused me with the importance of Catholic Social Teaching, often labelled "the Church's best-kept secret". The many notes, bibliographies and literature I accumulated helped greatly in the eventual composition of Unit 6 of the Life Light *Christian Morals* module which is devoted exclusively to Catholic Social Teaching and is currently studied by thousands of (mostly) teachers during their CCRS courses. I would hope that those who rightly mourn the passing of Plater might take comfort in the fact that, in a small way, the cause of CST continues to be served by distance learning.

The Methodist Church Open Learning Centre

In the mid-1990s, Roger Walton, Director of the Methodist Open Learning Centre in London, orchestrated the development of a distance-learning course on ecumenism. He invited input from the main Christian Churches and secured the cooperation of seven of them, including the Church of England, the Catholic Church, the Scottish Episcopalian Church, the Church of Ireland, the Salvation Army and the hosting Methodist Church. I was invited to join the working group which developed the project over the ensuing two years, 1995–7.

In the Introduction to the book which resulted from our efforts, Roger wrote: "You can imagine the fun we have had exchanging information and debating issues." There was indeed a most friendly, constructive and open-minded atmosphere throughout. We all learned from one another—more vividly than when we had been merely reading about each other. One instance in particular has taken root in my memory.

We were discussing the question of the Virgin Birth—was St Joseph the father of Jesus or was the Holy Spirit? The dialogue became animated and very academic with references to the Greek (Septuagint) translation of Isaiah 7:14 that Matthew 1:23 quotes when alluding to "the *virgin* (that) will conceive . . . ", whereas the original Hebrew text speaks merely of a "young woman" and cannot of itself bear the meaning attributed to it in Matthew 1:23. My own contribution detailed my recent review of *The Sacred Virgin and the Holy Whore* (Sphere Books, 1988) by Anthony Harris (no relation!) which affirmed that all documented cases of virgin births had been female, clones of their mothers. Hence, the author argued, Jesus was a woman, Luke 2:21 (the circumcision of Jesus) is spurious, and the Catholic Church should ordain women priests!

Amidst the hilarity, Laurie (who represented the Salvation Army) was unusually quiet and thoughtful. He was asked what the Army members thought. He replied: "You can think what you like—just so long as you get the soup up on time!"

This exchange has stayed with me. If, as in John 20:19–27, Jesus himself had appeared in the room at this point he would have smiled at all of us (I'm sure!). But he would surely have reserved a special smile for Laurie. Over the centuries, ecumenical dialogue has revolved around points of doctrine—ortho*doxy*. Perhaps we should transfer the emphasis to ortho*praxis* and examine our Christian practice: how we actually live out the gospel. Where there is a convergence of Christian practice and witness, could we not begin to take this as a basis for convergence of Christian identity? (See Chapter 13 for more on this line of thinking.)

Another benefit of taking part in this process was access to a tutorial for new distance-learning tutors. The programme was user-friendly, full of practical insights and very useful. All new Life Light postal tutors have taken part in this programme.

And then there was . . .

Of course, not all projects that we discussed with dioceses and centres came to fruition. In the summer of 1978, I sent details of our courses to Mgr George Leonard, Head of the Catholic Information Office in Abbots Langley. I was looking for a mention in *BRIEFING* (the Office's newsletter). He sent a kind and encouraging reply, adding that a mention in *BRIEFING* would indeed help us in our work. However, he added that "authoritative approval" would have to be obtained first.

I took up his suggestion and asked him how one would go about getting authoritative approval. He told me to write to Father Kelly (Secretary, Theology Commission) at Oscott College. I did this, enclosing a complimentary copy of our *Theology of Marriage*. (I thought that if he could "pass" this module—especially the section on the highly controversial encyclical *Humanae vitae*—he would have no difficulties with the rest!)

Father Kelly was a little upset at this request. "Why come to us? We are not an answering service, nor the Holy Office!" However, he liked the *Marriage* course, especially "the sensitive areas", which he thought reflected theology "as it actually is". He suggested approaching Bishop Hugh Lindsay (the bishop supervising the Information Office) for some sort of "recognition".

So I wrote to Bishop Lindsay, detailing the story so far and enclosing background information about Life Light, together with our *Marriage* module.

He replied in the negative: "I would have to do the same for all similar ventures." I returned to Mgr Leonard. He wrote that he was leaving the Information Office in a few days' time: would I contact his successor Father Hook? This I did on 13 July 1978.

No reply. Finally, on 27 July 1978, I phoned the Catholic Information Office. No one had ever heard of us!

I must admit that I was disappointed. But the passage of time has made me more understanding. As I review the pages of these letters to and fro, I now realize that it was a mistake to have selected *The Theology of Marriage* as the complimentary sample of our work. Our module took a somewhat critical stance on *Humanae vitae*—at the time a shibboleth of orthodoxy. This may well have provided George Leonard, Patrick Kelly, Bishop Lindsay and Father Hook with a problem. Recognizing us could well have been misinterpreted in Church circles—especially in the Vatican! Whatever the reason, the fact remains that the work Heather and I had done on marriage spirituality produced a different reaction from the positive response of members of the Church of England.

Then there were plans for courses in Brentwood and Portsmouth dioceses leading to the ordination of Permanent Deacons. These came to nothing—despite much enthusiasm from Bishop Worlock. A programme of cooperation with the Upholland Northern Institute was discussed with Father (later Cardinal) Vincent Nichols, but this was not taken further forward once the decision began to take shape in the late 1980s to close the site of this historic seminary.

A suggested Maryvale CRE course was dropped when it became clear that the Centre would be able to organize this for themselves. In 1992, preliminary talks took place in Newman College, Birmingham, with Martin O'Kane with a view to setting up a CCRS course. This too was abandoned. The College could well run its own course, as has proved to be the case under the very able directorship of Eamonn Elliott.

We were grateful to Brother Fillan for introducing Life Light to Father Joseph Chalmers, diocesan RE adviser in Glasgow. Bearsden College of Education was looking to set up a distance-learning course in theology in association with the University of Glasgow. A number of detailed meetings were held in the early 1990s. Nothing came of this project, although a successful Catholic Teachers' Certificate distance-learning course for teachers in Scotland was launched sometime later.

NBRIA, AARE and TEEF

Our work during the 1980s was greatly stimulated by our participation in three groups of like-minded RE providers. The National Board of Religious Inspectors and Advisers (NBRIA) hosted semi-annual conferences at which developments in especially school RE were discussed. More focused upon adult RE was the Association of Adult Religious Educators (AARE). As previously mentioned, this group originated in John Elias' Centre for Adult Religious Education at St Mary's, Strawberry Hill, and was efficiently developed by Anne McDowell, who became the first Chair. It operated by means of an annual conference and periodic newsletter. Heather and I offered to run the newsletter and did so between 1987 and 1991.

In 1988, I joined TEEF (Theological Education by Extension Forum) and attended a number of its conferences, often at its base in Oak Hill College, Southgate, London. Most often I was the only Catholic present: my contributions were therefore listened to (I thought) with a mildly embarrassing higher level of attention! I learned much from TEEF about the practicalities of postal tutoring.

One moment stands out in my memory more particularly, when Laurie Green led a workshop in the 1998 conference. We were discussing how to communicate with non-bookish course participants. Laurie reminded us of the fact that the greater part of Jesus' first audiences could neither read nor write. The first hearers of the Word for the most part *had* to be hearers. This is known as the "oralate" dimension of the Gospel texts. We learned that when talking about God, his relationship to me, the universe and all that exists, we have to analyse the language we use and that which the Bible uses.

The Bible was written mostly to be proclaimed in public to such oralate hearers. Ask any early years' teacher how s/he communicates with children who cannot as yet read: s/he will tell you that s/he uses drama, draws pictures and tells stories. Jesus does the same in the synoptic Gospels. He pictures beams of wood in the eyes of hypocrites, has camels attempting to go through the eye of a needle and so on. And he tells parables.

Oralates take on board new concepts in a way that is markedly different from the way we "literates" do. Oralates cannot retain abstract concepts, like greed, honour, wealth. This is why Jesus made such wide use in his parables of vivid, concrete images which his oralate hearers would have no difficulty remembering, like the *picture* of a camel trying to squeeze through the eye of a needle, or of a beam being removed from someone's eye, or of the actual removal of one's eye in certain circumstances.

We were encouraged to be sensitive to this when we interpreted biblical texts: we should not *necessarily* take literally words and phrases first uttered in an oralate setting. Fundamentalist readers of the Gospels sometimes take literally what was first uttered in an oralate context; for example, they search (in vain) for some Jerusalem gate that was so narrow that it was called "the eye of a needle".

I have ever since considered this a valid point. We should indeed put ourselves into the shoes of Confucius, Moses, Mohammed, Jesus or any ancient religious leader who wanted to talk to their followers about transcendental experiences. They all had that same problem! With very few exceptions, they would have been "oralate" and therefore had difficulty getting their heads round abstract ideas like "transcendence", "the beyond", etc.

One solution to this problem was to talk about a transcendental experience as an encounter with a *Person*—Shang-ti, Elohim, Allah, Father. This is personification—that is, where human features are ascribed to abstract ideas. It was widely used in the centuries before Jesus. Zeus and Jupiter personified governorship of the state; Mars personified the needs of war, and Venus those of sexuality, while the goddess Juno cared for women's concerns and so on.

In reality, this was a convention. The leaders were not saying that these "Persons" were persons in the sense that you and I are persons—that would have "miniaturized" the divinities! We too personify love relationships—think of Cupid with his bow.

Possibly through TEEF I was invited to a General Synod Board of Education conference at Church House, Westminster, held just before

Christmas in 1989 to probe the possibility of setting up a distance-learning course in theology leading to a degree. I was allowed a generous amount of time for my contribution in which I outlined the various programmes of theological distance learning in the Catholic Church internationally and in England.

From the early 1990s, we were to embark on the biggest project in the story of Life Light—the Catholic Certificate in Religious Studies (CCRS). I'll tell you about this in the next chapter.

10

The Catholic Certificate in Religious Studies

From early 1991, Bishop John Rawsthorne chaired a number of meetings of the Board of Religious Studies of the Bishops' Conference which had been called with a view to replacing the Certificate in Religious Studies (CRE). I described the CRE in Chapter 7 as well as Life Light's contribution to it. By the early nineties some problems had arisen with the CRE:

- The curriculum was being interpreted rather loosely by certain of the delivering diocesan and college authorities. Quality control presented problems.
- Increasingly, candidates who had enrolled found that, for a variety of reasons, they needed to transfer mid-course to other diocesan and college Centres. Given the diversity of approach taken by the various course deliverers, transfer was difficult. In most cases the Centres accepting such candidates required them to start their CRE course all over again.
- The CRE was only accessible to teachers. After the 1980 National Pastoral Congress, the need for courses for parish ministers had steadily grown, but they could not take the CRE course.

The Board presented the outline of a replacement course. It was to be called the Catholic Certificate in Religious Studies (CCRS).

- In contrast to the CRE, the new CCRS course would be modular in structure. There were to be eight self-standing modules. Six of these (*Hebrew Scriptures*, *Christian Scriptures*, *Christology*,

Church, *Sacraments* and *Christian Morals*) were to be called "core theology modules", deliverable to teachers and non-teachers alike. (These six modules reflected to a large extent the main curriculum areas of the traditional seminary course—except for Canon Law and Church History.) Two further modules were called "specialist modules". The content of the specialist modules varied according to the particular RE settings: school, parish, etc. The modules could in theory be worked through in any order.

- It would incorporate a transfer system whereby candidates who had satisfactorily completed one or more of the eight modules in one Centre could take those modules with them to their new Centre with no need to repeat them.
- It would become open to all—teachers and non-teachers alike.
- It would be overseen centrally—by the Board of Religious Studies of the Bishops' Conference. The Board alone would have the authority to issue final certificates.
- It set up a quality control system based upon regional moderation meetings.

By May 1991, the Board had published a set of "General Principles for the Delivery of the Course". The following month we made an official application to the Board for accreditation of Life Light as a Centre for the purposes of delivering the new course. In our application to the Board, I made reference to the increased need for alternative modes of CCRS delivery in view of the closure of several Catholic Training Colleges in the 1970s and 80s: Endsleigh College in Hull (1976), the Sisters of Charity College in Newbold Revel in Warwickshire (1978), the Religious of the Assumption's Maria Assumpta College in Kensington Square (1978), the De La Salle College at Hopwood Hall (1989), as well as others. From the very start of Hawkstone Hall Correspondence Courses, a large number of enquirers who had been adversely affected by these closures, and who were looking for alternatives, made contact with us. I have always thought that we were able to offer real and practical help here.

The Board's response was generally favourable to our application, although it made a number of observations. Complying with these kept Heather and myself very busy for the rest of 1991. However, the final package of our proposed modules was agreed at the Board's meeting of 30 January 1992, and we then received our accreditation.

The official start date of the new CCRS course was September 1992. Our own immediate task was to transfer our CRE course participants onto the new CCRS course. Because we have always had flexible enrolment—one might enrol and begin work at any point in the academic year—this was quite a complicated process, but Heather's patient eye for detail saw us through. As a result, we were ready to advertise the Life Light CCRS course from the summer of 1992. The diocese of Wrexham (and this is not widely appreciated) was the first diocese in England and Wales to have its CCRS course up and ready.

The start of the new academic year in 1992 marked a pleasing stage in the story of Life Light. Twenty years earlier, with the closure of Corpus Christi College in London, substantial courses in adult RE had become scarcer; now, with the inauguration of the CCRS, a two-year course, open to all over eighteen years of age, became available in every part of England and Wales. The CCRS was delivered in the Catholic colleges of education and in each of the twenty-two Catholic dioceses. With our own accreditation, it became possible for the CCRS to be worked through from home—no matter where one lived. More particularly, we had long argued that the CRE should be open to non-teachers; we had set up the Certificate in Adult RE (CARE) course to go some way to fill this gap. The CCRS had removed this problem: Life Light could now offer a course in adult RE leading to a certificate issued by the Board of Religious Studies on behalf of the Bishops' Conference.

All we had to do now was to ensure that we delivered the course efficiently and that we provided a meaningful period of study and reflection. The Life Light CCRS course established a number of features to enable this.

Features of the Life Light CCRS course

The process was by tutored distance learning and one group-discussion session in connection with each of the eight modules. Each module was sub-divided into six "units". All modules had the same features:

- *Reading.* The six units of each module were dispatched in accordance with a personal study programme, drawn up in accordance with each course participant's requirements. The units presented the issues for reflection following a system of programmed learning, in which one is offered the opportunity of proceeding systematically from experience to new awareness. Each unit consisted of written text, usually interfaced with a specific section of a course book, and interspersed with easily accessible "Reading Passages" (from the Bible, Vatican II passages, liturgical texts). For each module a bibliography was provided. This was divided into:
  - *Essential reading*: that is, the distance-learning course material, used in conjunction (usually) with an accessible course book.
  - *Supplementary reading*: a list of books meant to serve as a guide to any further study of particular points which a participant might wish to undertake at any time. It was not meant to convey the impression that each and every title had to be studied if one wanted to work through any particular module. These bibliographies directed the course participant to books which were more closely relevant to a particular unit in which s/he may have been interested.
- *Reflection.* Each unit concluded with a number of "Think-points". These had been designed to promote reflection upon the unit which had just been studied.
- *Problem raising.* At enrolment the participant was introduced to a series of postal tutors whose role it was to provide ongoing support while the module was being worked. The participant was also supplied with "Question Sheets". When s/he became aware of a problem in connection with a particular module, s/he was invited to formulate it as precisely as possible on a Question Sheet. Often the problem vanished at this point! But if it did not, s/he sent it to his/her postal tutor who would provide a written reply on the reverse side of the Question Sheet.
- *Written work.* The Think-points had also been worded in such a way as to stimulate a short essay. During any one module of the CCRS course, the participant was invited to select any one

Think-point and compose an essay of around 1,500 words on it. This essay was sent to his/her postal tutor who then evaluated it, made helpful and constructive comments and returned it.

- *Discussion.* Each module was discussed in facilitated small groups during one or other of two study weekends or at the summer school. Participants were invited to use their Question Sheets to send to the group facilitators the issues they wanted to discuss.
- *The Assessment*: This was mainly by essay. We initially followed an early Open University system of evaluation, in which the postal tutor made two assessments on each 1,500-word essay. Both were on a ten-point scale and indicated: (1) the breadth of content of the essay; (2) the degree of comprehension of the main themes of the module. These evaluations were communicated both to the participant and to Life Light. Participants who gained at least 50 per cent of the marks available for a module were awarded one credit. In borderline cases or where a participant's engagement level was in doubt, participation in group discussion was also taken into account.
- *Flexible enrolment:* As with all Life Light courses, the CCRS course (or any individual module) could be begun at any point in the year, including vacation periods. These free-standing modules could be taken in any order.

The course materials for each of the eight CCRS modules were completed by 1992. Thereafter the texts were subject to constant revision—based upon the reactions, observations and corrections of the participants, as well as the ongoing developments in theology and RE. In this way, the presentations have always been fresh and, hopefully, user-friendly for our many course participants.

And there have indeed been many course participants! Between 1992 and 2021, we have registered some 4,229 course participants for the CCRS and applied to the Board for final certificates in respect of some 3,112 who had successfully completed their courses. In addition, we have welcomed hundreds of students who have transferred to us from the Centre or College at which they originally enrolled.

Why would they transfer? Typically, a trainee teacher enrolled locally for a two-year CCRS course to run alongside their one-year PGCE course, thus requiring some other Centre where they might work through their remaining modules. If they applied to Life Light, we would draw up a tailor-made programme starting immediately which would incorporate the modules needed and which would see them through to final certification. A large number of CCRS graduates have indicated to us that, had it not been for Life Light, they would not have been able to complete their CCRS course and consequently their teaching careers would have taken a different course.

Our postal tutors

We could not have accomplished this without the invaluable support of our excellent team of postal tutors. In the early days postal tutors tended to supply their services for rather short periods before being called away to other forms of educational service. Daniel O'Leary and Teresa Sallnow tutored the catechetical module they had written. Sister Patricia England OP tutored the *Sacraments* module until being called away to Norway. We were grateful also to Sister Laurentia Ayling of the Westminster RE Centre, Ann Barton, Sr Dolores Dodgson RA and Nancy Roberts. Jimmy Mythen designed and tutored a module on New Testament Greek.

However, once we had settled into the CCRS, our tutors stayed longer. The most outstanding contributions have come from Sister Alexia Morris (*Sacraments/Religious Life*), Peter McCafferty (*Hebrew Scriptures/RE*), Alan Geary (*Church/Morals*) and Susan Kowal (*Christian Scriptures/ Sacraments*). Together they have provided tutor support for a good proportion of those 3,000 successful CCRS candidates, considering, evaluating and giving advice on some 18,000 essays!

Summer schools and study days

During the five-day summer schools at St Mary's and the two study weekends in Llandudno, course participants had the opportunity to meet, share insights, socialize and take part in meaningful liturgy. The actual format of these get-togethers changed and developed over the years. The first of them, in 1979, was strictly speaking a summer school of St Mary's; there was minimal reference to the home-study modules. So long as there was a prestigious speaker (such as Tom Groome, Gabriel Moran, Mary Boys, Paddy Purnell, Mary Grey, Daniel O'Leary, Duncan Macpherson, Peter McCaffrey) in attendance, there was little incentive to discuss the modules!

Gradually this changed. With the tightening of procedures of the CRE, and especially of the CCRS, provision was increasingly made to enable a review and discussion of each of the modules. At first the idea was to discuss modules that had *already* been studied at home. Later we started getting evaluation returns which indicated that most participants would welcome a change: instead of discussing material already covered, they would prefer sessions which *introduced* the various modules before the period of home study. So we made the change.

Working with the diocese of Derry

The early years of our summer schools in the 1980s were remarkable for one constant feature in particular: the large number of trainee teachers who had travelled from Northern Ireland to Strawberry Hill specifically to take part in the summer school. They did so as part of their CRE/CCRS courses. Members of the RS department at St Mary's frequently observed that many of the issues being discussed at summer school at that time were not relevant to the RE setting in Northern Ireland. For example, during the 1980s, there was much concentration on how to teach world religions, on multifaith issues and multicultural pedagogy—themes which were to become live issues in Ireland only at a later stage. However, schools in Northern Ireland insisted that applicants for posts in Catholic schools should be in possession of some form of Catholic

Teachers' Certificate. The Life Light CRE/CCRS course was one way these students could get their "piece of paper".

In 1989, Bishop Edward Daly of Derry sought our help in solving this problem. Courses leading to a Catholic Teachers' Certificate were few and far between in Northern Ireland at that time and involved regular long journeys—usually to St Mary's, Belfast. Many trainee teachers were reluctant to make the journey, especially during the dark evenings. Moreover, this was the time of the Troubles—you may recall the historic image of a priest waving a bloodstained white handkerchief while he ministered to the dead and dying on the streets of Derry on Sunday, 30 January 1972. That heroic priest was to become Bishop Daly of Derry. He now wondered whether our CRE course could help with his trainee teachers' problem.

So on 13 February 1991, I took the night boat from Stranraer to Larne en route for a meeting in Derry with Father Tony Mailey, the RE Adviser for the diocese. The diesel train from Belfast to Derry took root at Bellarena, the final station before Derry. The engine had flooded. A lady opposite to me took out her rosary. The driver free-wheeled the train into the winter sunshine. I unpacked my conference papers and started to plan a way of transforming our five-day Strawberry Hill Summer School programme into a double study weekend format. I completed the rough draft within the hour—just as the diesel train burst into life (and the lady gratefully returned her rosary to her bag). The new format thereafter became known in Derry circles as "the Bellarena format"!

The minutes of this 1991 meeting indicate a very full discussion. We were helped by Jo McGuinness, Tony Mailey's secretary, who was to prove an invaluable asset during the years that followed. A Life Light Centre was set up within the diocese of Derry and a programme of study weekends was drawn up, starting in 1992. These initially took place in the diocesan RE Centre in Termonbacca on the outskirts of Derry, overlooking the beautiful Foyle river. Later we moved to the Drummond Hotel in Ballykelly (which boasted an oratory in addition to its many other pleasing features). Finally, we made use of the Thornhill Centre on the Culmore Road. Candidates were now able to enrol for the CCRS and work through all aspects of it without leaving Ireland.

A further development took place in 2006. One of the participants of our study day in October 2004 was Monica Byrne. She had set off in her car from Aughrim, Co. Wicklow just after four in the morning, arriving at the Thornhill Centre in time for registration at 9.30. She took an active part in the day and contributed much. After the final session at 6.00 pm she began her long drive home to Co. Wicklow. She told me that, of all the options open to her to acquire a Teachers' Certificate, this was the only one that was in any way feasible.

Monica's dedication touched my heart. From the beginning of our operation in Derry, there had always been interest from the Republic of Ireland. This was natural: the border with the Republic was only a few miles from the Thornhill Centre. However, candidates began to enrol from all over Ireland. To cut a long story short, with the much-appreciated help of Father John Byrne OSA of the Orlagh Retreat Centre near Dublin, study days started in this historic setting from summer 2006, thereby cutting many journey times.

Meanwhile Tony Mailey, with the help of Maura Hyland (author of the "Alive O!" programme for primary schools), customized the CCRS course for Ireland. This was done by a special module entitled *RE in the Primary School in Ireland.* There were questions raised about the recognition of the CCRS in both Northern Ireland and throughout Ireland, but these were sorted out amicably with the help of Bishop John Rawsthorne.

CCRS in the Middle East

The CCRS was set up by the Board of Studies for use in England and Wales. However, from the start it attracted interest from around the English-speaking world, notably Ireland, the United States, Australia and New Zealand. Representatives from these countries have on occasions been welcomed to take part in meetings of the Board and at CCRS conferences. Life Light operates in distance-learning mode and so is well placed to further this interest. The Board gave us permission to deliver the CCRS outside the dioceses of England and Wales, provided that the Church authorities concerned were agreeable.

In 1998, we were approached by the Apostolic Vicariate of Southern Arabia. The then Vicar General, Father Francis Jamieson, took me to lunch at the Athenaeum in London where we discussed and planned a CCRS course for members of the cathedral parish of Abu Dhabi. According to the plan, we would supply the course materials and the postal-tutor support and Father Francis organized the regular group meetings to discuss each module.

At the conclusion of the course, I presented seventeen successful CCRS candidates with their well-earned certificates during Mass in the cathedral on 22 February 2003. Liturgy in the Middle East can be quite lively! We had 800 English-speaking Indians, Filipinos, Arabs, ex-pats from everywhere—all in full voice. And they all applauded loudly as each of the seventeen approached the altar for his/her certificate! There was a party afterwards, and another one the following day—finishing with a feast in a quayside fish restaurant and a boat trip in the Gulf. I was presented with a very expensive carpet which still enhances my bedroom. The CCRS graduates were formed into a catechetical group with a particular interest in adult RE. It continues to provide a useful ministry.

The return flight was quite fraught. The Iraq War was looming and British Airways cancelled my 2.15 am flight to London at very short notice. I was transferred to a KLM flight to Amsterdam and spent six hours at Schiphol Airport awaiting a BA flight to Heathrow.

On to the Board of Studies

At the November Board meeting of the following year, 2004, it was suggested and agreed that Life Light should join the Board of Studies, alongside representatives from the colleges and dioceses. At the time the Chair was Father (later Monsignor) Andrew Faley, with Father Des Seddon as Secretary. Andrew has a well-earned reputation as a first-class facilitator of meetings, as I had already experienced during his skilful handling of NBRIA and AARE meetings and conferences.

I recall him once telling me what Board of Studies meetings had been like a few years previously. There would be two sessions. In the morning the executive group (mostly clergy) would meet, discuss and decide issues on an agenda. In the afternoon the Chair would hold a separate meeting of the non-executives (mostly laity) who would work through the same agenda and learn of the decisions already taken in the morning. By 2004, all that had changed and there was now a single meeting.

Before my first meeting, I was apprehensive at the sort of reception I could expect—especially as an ex-priest! I really need not have worried. Thanks largely to Andrew, there was always a calm, purposeful and constructive atmosphere with the occasional oasis of hilarity. This was very successfully continued under Andrew's successor, Des Seddon.

Over the years we discussed many issues—usually over a number of sessions:

- The academic level at which the CCRS should be delivered: should this be Level 3 or Level 4? (We eventually decided on Level 4, roughly the level at which first-year undergraduate courses at university are delivered.)
- Should we seek accreditation from some academic body, possibly with a view to securing financial support? (In the end we left this to the local Centres.)
- Ongoing quality control, especially as regards the regular moderation meetings of the various provinces, discerning plagiarism and ways of indicating attainment (on the last point we fixed on the Distinction-Pass-Fail model).
- Administration procedures, especially concerning registration and certification, etc, etc.

Developments in distance learning: E-learning

Back in 1974, when I was setting up Hawkstone Hall Correspondence Courses, there was a fair amount of scepticism about the credibility of distance learning. The received wisdom at the time was that the ideal setting for learning to be satisfactorily achieved was face to face. By the turn of the millennium, this attitude had changed due to a number of factors: the advent of computers, telecommunications improvements, the more extensive use of video and recording facilities and so on. There were also steady improvements in the techniques of delivering courses by distance learning and in the quality of course materials.

From 2000, we were sometimes asked if we had considered replacing our hard-copy materials by online programmes. We took this seriously, and I recall spending long hours trying to get my head around Moodle (the acronym for "Modular object-oriented dynamic learning environment"—a widely-used e-learning programme) and its possible application to Life Light.

Then the Board of Studies accepted a proposal from Ushaw College to develop an online version of the CCRS. From 2004 it was delivered under the direction of Dr Ros Stuart-Buttle and provided the alternative format for which some course participants were looking. I immediately removed the wet towel from my head, welcomed this new development and offered the new project support in a number of ways. Life Light would henceforth offer a service that was complementary to the Ushaw online CCRS programme. Our distance-learning clients would now have more choice. Ushaw College closed in 2011 and the online CCRS course transferred to Liverpool Hope University.

The end of the study days

The new online CCRS course did not include periodic get-togethers. Over the years, the Life Light study day system made a significant contribution to the overall "home study + study day" formula. Many student evaluations witnessed to wide appreciation of the study day, especially in terms of motivation raising: a number of students submitted their first essay only *after* their study day.

However, other student evaluations began to reflect a changing, more negative attitude. We adopted the "home study + study day/study weekend/summer school" structure in the late 1970s. The model, as we have seen, was the Open University. In the interim much had changed. Technology had developed out of all recognition. In the 1970s, communication relied mainly on the postal services, whereas now we had enhanced telephonics, email, the net. Student and tutor-student interactivity now took place in settings other than the study day. By 2005, distance learning was far more widely practised—even by university curriculum deliverers. Every CCRS candidate had had some experience of distance learning before enrolling with us. One purpose of the study day had been to introduce course participants to the technicalities and procedures of distance learning. This was no longer needed.

CCRS course participants had far less leisure to attend study days than in the leisurely 1970s—when the PGCE was commonly experienced as a breathing space after the rigours of the final degree examinations and before the commencement of one's teaching. Consequently it had become increasingly difficult to identify dates which were convenient for PGCE students, especially in the case of those working from overseas. The numbers of "no shows" increased notably after 2000. Non-attendees were debarred from receiving their final CCRS certificates, and the fear was that these teachers might be lost to Catholic education.

The study day had become expensive. With their own costs constantly rising, Centres had had to increase their charges to accommodate us. Travelling to our Centres had become more costly as well. Unless one lived close to a Centre, the study day hit the student's pocket disproportionately hard, by comparision with the cost of the home-study section of the course.

Finally, we were having increasing difficulties securing the services of a priest to celebrate the Eucharist—always a central feature at our get-togethers which promoted the community aspect of the occasion. Participants who had never met one another before felt that the shared liturgy helped to transform them into a group. However, priests were fully occupied at weekends—and our study days just had to be at weekends. For all these reasons we reluctantly took the decision in 2008 to terminate the study days.

Twenty-five years on

CCRS Online would not have developed but for the drive, initiative and professional expertise of Dr Ros Stuart-Buttle. She had been awarded a doctorate by Liverpool Hope University for her research work into e-learning, and she shared her expertise with the Board of Studies and CCRS course deliverers on numerous occasions.

In 2019, Ros published a 100-page research paper for the Bishops' Conference on the first twenty-five years of the CCRS.[1] This document contains methodically gathered data and faithful accounts of professionally held interviews involving both course participants and deliverers. As such it is a valuable resource of detailed information about the CCRS—its history, statistics, course participants' evaluations, course-deliverers' experiences and much more.

Just under 30,000 applicants have registered with the Board for the CCRS since 1992. Of these, some 13,500 successfully completed their courses and received their certificates. The Life Light contribution to these figures is 4,229 registrations and 3,112 certificates.

I was much heartened to read on page 8 of the report that 83 per cent of respondents stated that their course had "met or surpassed their expectations" and that 89 per cent considered the course relevant to today's world and that they would recommend the course to others. This finding tallies with our own experience at Life Light. The vast majority of new enrolments have come from personal recommendations. (We have not had to advertise for many years!)

CCRS Twenty-five Years On is a carefully balanced document. Alongside the positive points that emerged from the research, much space is devoted to noting the reservations that the contributors expressed about their experiences. Some found the content too theological. Some looked for greater interface with the classroom. Others opined that the CCRS tries to do too much, intending as it does to provide a service to a wide spectrum of previous academic attainment. The report's sub-title is significant—"One Size Fits All?"

A list of fourteen recommendations towards the end of the document indicates how the CCRS might be improved. The Board has pledged to consider these and, where advised, to act upon them. Life Light will willingly implement where possible any suggestions for improving its delivery of the CCRS.

The story of Life Light Home Study Courses clearly owes much to the CCRS and to the Board of Studies. From that sleepless hot summer night in Brussels in 1973, through changing times and circumstances, I have constantly sought ways to promote adult religious education. Working collaboratively with the Board over the past thirty years has increased our course participant numbers dramatically, enabled many thousands of mostly young Catholics to raise their levels of biblical and theological literacy, and contributed to the effectiveness of their teaching ministry.

That's a lot of man/woman hours of effort, study and reflection on their part!

11

Domestic Bliss

"The Christian of the future will be a mystic or will not exist at all."[1] Christopher Lamb made use of this quote to convey the thinking of one of the most influential theologians of the twentieth century: Karl Rahner. Rahner forecast an age of Christian spirituality when we would experience God within "the very heart of our existence"—and no longer exclusively in the desert, convent or monastery. In Chapter 8, I set out to show how this shift of emphasis from cloister to hearth has been one feature of the story of Heather and myself—and indeed of Life Light.

Etienne Gilson (1884–1978) wrote of a *paradisus claustralis* in his work on the mystical theology of St Bernard of Clairvaux (1090–1153), founder of the Cistercian Order.[2] To understand this concept we must first recall that we have been made in the image and likeness of God. For Bernard, the "image" referred to the fact that we have been given free will; the "likeness" was a reference to the orderly motions of that free will. Through monastic self-denial and mortification the *dis*orderly motions of our free will—the result of Adam's Fall—may be *re*ordered to become once again in harmony with our original "likeness" to God. When this is achieved, God is thought to recognize himself in us, and so we become worthy of his love. From that point on, we love God, and we love ourselves *only* for God's sake. For Bernard, this was the highest level of divine love that is possible for humankind. It was acommpanied by a deep peace—*paradisus claustralis.*

The period of time which followed our marriage in 1977 I would describe as *paradisus domesticus* ("domestic paradise" or "homely bliss"—as distinct from *paradisus claustralis*). To understand this, recall that God made us in his own image and likeness—"male and female he created them" (Genesis 1:26–7). We are *already* like God in our maleness and femaleness, already loved, already smiled on, especially as we extend his human family or attend to its wellbeing.

I treasure my diaries, souvenirs, photo albums, cards and memorabilia from the 1980s onwards. Anyone examining them from the outside would see (apart from the various Life Light developments which I have described in the last four chapters) a fairly ordinary sequence of family events: the arrivals of Phil and Liz and their upbringing, moving house, parish events, the weddings of family members, holidays, birthdays, bereavements, loving funerals of deceased pets. But for Heather and me each event seemed to be being lived at a deeper level—under the smile of God. We were leading very busy lives, but they were orderly lives and free from stress. (I would love to have shared our experience with Karl Rahner!)

The point I wish to make here is that I think that *anybody* can experience *paradisus domesticus.* Unless you really want to, there is no need to hang holy pictures all over the home, nor to emphasize the externals of piety. It is the ordinary tasks of life, performed well and with love, that bring us close to God. It is the loving relationship with our life partner that (to use St Bernard's line of thinking) enables God to recognize himself in us. Just by living and working together we are living lives that are "in tune" with the meaning of life—whatever that is! In religious terms, we live continually in conformity to the will of God who created us like this and took satisfaction from what he had created (cf. Genesis 1:31). Ordinary living makes us worthy of his love and so we experience a deep-down peace.

It's a girl!!

The 1980s were a busy time for Life Light. But family life proceeded apace too! On 15 May 1981, Heather and I were watching the evening news and learned that Zara Phillips had arrived in the household of Princess Anne and Mark Phillips. We had had two false alarms with Heather's second pregnancy, but it must have been the news about Zara that finally got things going. Shortly after midnight—panic stations! Heather was sure that we were "minutes away" from increasing the number of our family.

Heather was installed in the back seat of our Ford Anglia, and off we went to the John Radcliffe Hospital in Oxford, some fifteen miles away.

"Can we go a little faster?" Heather kept on saying. (Usually it was "Can we go a little slower?") I drove as smoothly and as fast as I could. There was a sense of urgency in the back of the car: would we make the John Radcliffe in time? All went well until just before the Pear Tree Roundabout in Oxford which is about two miles from the hospital. It was two o'clock in the morning on 16 May. I was suddenly confronted by a solid block of motorbikes on the A40, occupying both sides of the carriageway, and doing a steady 10 mph. I wound down my window—to be comforted by "Peace, Man!" issuing from a large growth of facial hair. "Never any need to rush! Slow down! Peace . . . !"

"A baby is being born on my back seat!" I screamed.

"Sh*t! Follow me!"

And this peaceful young biker cleared a path for us and sped us to the John Radcliffe. Before I had time to park and get into reception, Liz had graced us with her presence!

We had chosen not to enquire about the sex of our next born. We Harrises normally produce boys. My Dad was the eldest of four boys; his Dad was the eldest of four boys and three girls. During the twentieth century we had produced only one girl, my niece Marian.

So it was an immense joy to welcome Liz, our first girl for twenty-seven years! My Mum, who by this time had moved into a bungalow opposite our house, was particularly excited at the prospect of having a granddaughter so near. I had the distinct impression that, in her eyes, I had *finally* justified my existence. She now had the baby girl she always wanted! Her final years—she died aged eighty-three in 1986—were spent in the joy and fulfilment of having her immediate family close by.

Bringing up Philip and Liz was a joy. We often assured them that "You gave us an easy ride!" With the experience of having worked on our Theology of Marriage module, we were able to live out our family life under the smile of God. Not that we were especially pious, as I have said. We never went in for the family rosary, for example. But the innumerable little things we did for Phil and Liz we saw as pertaining to the spiritual life. In the monastery, I used to serve the community members at table. I did so as a feature of my spiritual life. Now I would lay a table for the family with a similar mindset: this was a minuscule component in the process of ongoing creation. As such it was God's work, an *opus Dei.* In those days, I would wash up; nowadays I would change a nappy and so on. The gospel values of the cloister were in this way transferred to the setting of the hearth. In our enthusiasm, we wrote a couple of articles in 1982 for Daniel O'Leary's *NEW REview* on pre-school catechetics. These were "Toddling to God" and "Isn't he just like his Daddy!"

Holidays—just a few snapshots

In the early days, our family holidays always revolved around the needs of Phil and Liz. (Heather and I thought that we could not settle down and relax unless and until the kids were happy.) So we booked in to Butlin's Holiday Camps in Minehead, Pwllheli and Brighton, with their unlimited rides in the fun fair and much else. We appreciated the chalet patrol, which provided parents of young children with the freedom to visit the theatre, cinema or have a meal. If your child started to cry, this was flagged up where you were. However, one night we went to a concert in camp. The music was doubtless appropriate to the clientele, but Heather and I found it a bit too loud. We played noughts and crosses on the back of our Butlin's receipt and resolved that the first "crying child" would be ours!

In connection with Butlin's, I must own up to telling a lie to my son. The annual fun fair was taking place in nearby Chipping Norton. Phil was very keen to be taken there, whereupon I told him a lie—the only lie I ever told him: "The Chippy Fun Fair is only for people not rich enough to go to Butlin's!"

Having eventually graduated from Butlin's, we Eurocamped in Brittany and the Vendée for two summer family holidays. The next stage was a number of package holidays to Crete, Turkey and Greece. After that Phil and Liz began to make their own holiday arrangements, leaving Heather and me free to indulge our own interests a little more. We toured the Holy Land, Luxor, Canada (on the Rocky Mountaineer train), Austria, Switzerland, Germany and Scandinavia. We also visited Rome and Dubai.

During the very hot summer of 2003 we visited Taizé. We had made no holiday arrangements by July of that year. We took a last-minute decision to simply get in the car, take the ferry to Cherbourg and spend a fortnight getting lost in France. Taizé was the farthest point of our meanderings. For me, it was a return to a precious spot from which I had derived much inspiration during my Lumen Vitae course in 1976. A high point during our short stay was the Sunday Eucharist attended by (literally) hundreds of mostly young folks from different countries and denominations. An announcement was made before the entry procession to the effect that six Catholic bishops from England who had been making a retreat during the previous week would be concelebrating the Eucharist. Heather and I were eager to find out who our bishops were—but we were too far from the altar to be able to see. The distribution of Communion was a moving experience, a vivid demonstration of unity in diversity. Later, though, over coffee Heather asked me why I was so pensive.

I had recently attended a meeting of the National Board of RE Instructors and Advisers (NBRIA). There had been a session devoted to our Bishops' Conference 1998 publication "One Bread One Body"—which (among other things) reiterated the ban on eucharistic hospitality. Non-Catholics were not to be admitted to Communion at Catholic Eucharists. Yet here—and after a week of prayer—our good bishops had shown how "One Bread One Body" could work out in practice. Good on them! Heather fell in love with Taizé. When the founder Frère Roger was assassinated there in 2005, we both returned for his funeral.

Continuing a practice from early girlhood, Heather kept a diary throughout these trips. With the passage of time these travelogues make for stimulating reading. Most of our European holidays were based upon point-to-point rail trips. (Yes, she was indulging me!) Poignantly as we passed through Liège in Belgium on one occasion, she noted that "this was where Chris decided to marry me". (Well . . . it was *something* like that.)

We both enjoyed classical music, and we made a point of spending time in locations with musical associations: Bonn (Beethoven), Salzburg/Vienna (Mozart), Leipzig (Bach, Schumann) and Bergen (Grieg). Forever after, whenever we heard the works of these composers, we were pleasantly reminded of our holidays.

Heather harvested an enormous number of teaching aids on these journeys: the Frauenkirche in Dresden (wartime links with Coventry Cathedral), memorabilia from the Holy Land, stunning scenic vistas from everywhere. Our day in Martin Luther's Wittenberg she appreciated greatly. We visited the castle church on whose door Luther famously nailed his ninety-five theses against indulgence-selling Tetzel in 1517. We studied these over coffee. She had no problems with the spring-cleaning of Reconciliation and the prioritizing of the Scriptures! What was all the fuss about? She also liked the detail that one of the first tasks of Mrs Luther after their marriage in 1525 was to take all his clothes and give them a good wash. Then she deloused his cat!

I learned a little about attitudes to death in the Middle Ages during our 1993 holiday in Castelnaudary in southern France. Phil and I visited the Musée de Torture in the walled town of Carcassonne. Reading a helpful pamphlet under the gigantic guillotine near the entrance I got a fresh perspective into the background to the familiar "Eternal rest give unto them, O Lord . . . " of our funeral liturgy. It appears that there was a pervasive phobia of departed souls returning to haunt the living, to settle scores and so on. The "eternal *rest*" that was requested was partly that the deceased could rest peacefully in their graves and not bother those they had left behind!

We both took a particular delight in reliving Gospel experiences: sitting in the amphitheatre in Efes (Ephesus), looking down the main street of the town and reading John 1:1–14 while trying to discern the impact of those words upon the first hearers in the town. We reread the Sermon on the Mount on the "mount" itself—it's really only a hill! And we spent a long time in Jerusalem.

We also visited Ireland many times. We sometimes took the opportunity afforded by the study weekends in Derry and Dublin to enjoy short breaks in places like the Giant's Causeway and Glendalough. Heather's mum Noreen was born and raised on the west coast of Ireland—at Bonniconlon, Co. Mayo to be precise—and so there was, and is, a large family circle living on both the east and west coasts. These required frequent visiting. In this way, we covered most of the counties of Ireland and have many happy memories of them all. In the Vale of Avoca, Co. Wicklow, Noreen and I sang "The Meeting of the Waters" under the very tree where Thomas Moore (1779–1852) composed it. Noreen is no Mary O'Hara,[3] and it took us a little time to settle down to our duet. The problem was that, whereas I thought I knew the tune of "The Meeting of the Waters", Noreen sang it lustily to "The Mountains of Mourne". (The result will be a long time reaching Number One in the charts!)

Family bliss

Heather and I brought up Phil and Liz while we worked together on the projects described in the previous chapters. We had two desks in a small office where there was not a square inch to spare. Our friends used to comment: "God—you two must be in love! You are never apart 24/7!" It wasn't difficult. Heather routinely put me first; I routinely put her first. And we both put Phil and Liz first.

We both had experience of religious life before we met. As I described earlier, in the course of researching our *Theology of Marriage* module, we both came to discover the theological foundations of married and family spirituality. We tried in our daily life to put our new insights into practice. At first, we would recite sections of the Divine Office together. Later this gave way to less formal ways of praying together, as we developed the mindset of living in the presence of God. Procreators ourselves, we felt close to the Creator, the God of Life. We shared our joys and challenges. We both appreciated Daniel O'Leary's sessions on Incarnational Theology at St Mary's and progressively contemplated God in everything—in working together on Life Light, in the prosaic details of daily life, and especially in each other and our children.

From adolescence, I periodically experienced the absence of God, which I have described in the preceding chapters. The writing of my thesis on "How to talk to the modern adult about God" was therapeutic to the extent that it clarified my thinking. But it was not until I discovered how Jesus himself contemplated God—as an all-pervading Presence—that I found peace of mind. And this was deepened significantly from the moment I began to share that Presence with Heather.

When he was about eight, Phil had his first spiritual crisis. He had been longing for snow all through the Christmas holidays. On his second day back at school, he became truly desperate and was espied praying very earnestly in his room: "Lord, for God's sake let's have some snow!" Next morning Milton-under-Wychwood was cut off by snow-blocked roads. Nothing moved except the odd tractor. There was no school. Snowmen beamed cheerfully as snowball battles raged over a wide theatre of war.

Our own little soldier reported back for lunch scarred, bruised, rosy-cheeked, soaked—but happy. BBC *News at One* was reporting chaos in Kent, road accidents, a rail snow plough itself buried in snow, plus the customary widespread misery. The happy face became increasingly alarmed. " . . . Xpect they'll blame *me* for all this!" he muttered apprehensively.

His sister could manifest altruistic tendencies as well. As part of our family table liturgy one Sunday, we opened a bottle of 1985 Liebfraumilch. Liz, then aged eight, looked concerned. She knew that she herself would not be getting any wine—but then that was not what was troubling her. She confided her problem to Heather: "Mummy don't drink any of that!"

"Why ever not, darling?" Heather gently enquired.

"Just look at that label. It's way past its sell-by date!"

Our families, our parish, our village, our Life Light work—all made for a fulfilling social life. At the time, we agreed never to trumpet the happiness of our married life. The downside of this agreement was, of course, that we could not spread the joy and fulfilments of what we had discovered and were experiencing. As we have seen, this dilemma faces many spiritually-minded marrieds.

Heather and I played an active part in our Holy Trinity parish in Chipping Norton. While we were parishioners, the parish was run by the Jesuits under Father Tom Middlehurst. This meant that we enjoyed a wide selection of Mass homilies, as members of the Society made their short visits. Memorable in this context were the periodic sermons from Father Rodger Charles, who popularized Catholic Social Teaching, and Father Alfred Buttigieg, who taught Mathematics at Oxford University. They were following in the footsteps of Father (later Cardinal) John Carmel Heenan and Father (later Archbishop) George Patrick Dwyer—both of whom as young priests delivered missions at Holy Trinity.

I was voted on to the Parish Council at the meeting of 30 April 1984, and later became its Chair. While on the council I set up a discussion group, produced a parish directory and in 1988 organized a five-page questionnaire for parishioners to express how they felt about the way the council was running their parish. Most of the findings were predictable—except this one: "Would you like to see more cooperation with members of other denominations, or less?" Of those who replied "more" (50 per cent), a third of them spontaneously expressed the wish to be allowed "to go to each other's services".

Back to school

I referred just now to Heather collecting visual aids for her teaching. She taught at St George Napier Secondary School in Banbury shortly after we got married. She began maternity leave after a year, and decided to continue it through the years of raising Phil and Liz and through the hectic years of Life Light's development. Then in 1994, with Phil aged sixteen and Liz fourteen, she accepted an invitation from Sister Mary Dominic, Head of St Clotilde's girls' school in Lechlade, Oxfordshire, to return to teaching. (Heather had to consider this carefully. Among other issues to ponder, Liz was a pupil at the school!)

The Order running Liz's school was founded in France by Madame Antoinette Desfontaines (1760–1821). Amidst the religious confusion of post-Revolution France, she saw a way in which the Faith could survive, namely by educating the daughters of the remaining well-heeled sections of society. The Sisters took the title of the Congregation of St Clotilde. (St Clotilde (c. 470–545) was the wife of Clovis, the pagan founder of the Merovingian dynasty, whom Clotilde persuaded to convert to Christianity. His very public baptism encouraged the spread of Christianity throughout the Frankish kingdom. From that point on, France became a Catholic country.) The Sisters set up a number of girls' schools throughout France. When they were expelled from France to surrounding countries at the beginning of the twentieth century, they eventually set up a school within Lechlade Manor in 1939.

Heather joined the teaching staff in September 1994. We both grew to love the Sisters. Unlike many religious orders, which had been founded to teach the poor and whose current members agonized over the fact that they were now teaching the rich, the Sisters of St Clotilde were spared such identity crises. Around the time that Heather started teaching in Lechlade, I myself was invited to join the Board of Governors. In 1996, Heather became headteacher—no connection with my governorship! This involved frequent meetings for both of us at the mother house in Paris in the rue de Reuilly, and we became good customers of the recently introduced Eurostar train.

In common with many convent schools from the 1970s on (including Heather's own old school in Rise in Yorkshire), St Clotilde's experienced falling numbers of students and consequently steadily rising financial problems. The governing body worked overtime to reverse this trend, but we were increasingly aware that we would not succeed where so many other similar convent schools had failed. To cut a long story short, a chapter meeting of the Sisters in Paris in June 1998 decreed that St Clotilde's would close at the end of the current academic year—five weeks later.

At a Paris meeting of headteachers held earlier, in January 1998, Heather had been assured that no decision on St Clotilde's was imminent and that all GCSE and A level courses would be completed before any closure. On this basis, Heather and the teaching staff had been continuing their programmes and planning.

Domestic bliss was severely tested! We were both resigned to the fact that this was how decisions were often taken in religious life: a culture of secrecy before the point of decision, followed by a "no arguments" implementation. It helped our peace of mind that we were able to see the bigger picture. We resolved to accept reality and to do a first-class job on the closure of a dearly loved school.

At least Heather had the advantage of being married to a former headmaster who had also been ordered to close his school. At that time, I prided myself that I had secured a place in alternative schools for every single Juvenist. No boy suffered serious disruption to his education. Heather now faced the same task. We worked together on this—events, liturgical and social, to mark the closure, cooling tempers, dissuading legal action—as well as everything else involved in winding up a school. We accomplished both by March 1999.

One of the students who had to be found alternative provision was our own daughter. By July 1998 she had completed only the first year of her two-year A level course. After a not-too-straightforward set of negotiations, she began a one-year tailor-made course of study at Oxford Tutorial College to see her through to the end of her A levels. Thereafter she passed to Oxford Brookes University and graduated with honours in July 2002.

Heather enrolled in Westminster College in Oxford for a Teachers' Professional Course. This led to a B. Phil (Education) from the University of Warwick in 2001. During this course she was approached by St Joseph's Sister of Mercy School in Kenilworth, Warwickshire, which was looking for a new Head. We thought hard. Another convent school? Another possibility of closure? Some of the staff at St Joseph's expressed the fear that Heather was being appointed as a tried-and-tested convent school terminator.

Heather took over as Head in September 1999, and very quickly settled into her new challenge. She was well received by the teaching staff and the governing body and was relieved to hear that there were few financial worries. St Joseph's was a 4–18 day-school, coeducational up to eleven, girls only thereafter. She had a regular teaching slot in the senior school. At times, she was also called upon to take some primary school lessons. This was a new experience for her; her PGCE was secondary orientated, but she found it refreshing to face a different set of educational challenges.

She was soon involved in discussions with nearby Princethorpe College with a view to a possible merger with her 11–18 girls. This took place in September 2001, and Heather became Deputy Head at Princethorpe to John Shinkwin. Thereafter St Joseph's, renamed Crackley Hall, continued as a 4–11 junior school for boys and girls.

And so it was that the Harris family made contact again with Princethorpe. The Benedictine Sisters had now moved out to a smaller priory in Fernham, Oxfordshire. In 1966, they had sold Princethorpe to the Missionaries of the Sacred Heart, who then transferred their school in Leamington Spa to this much more spacious site. By the turn of the millennium, it was flourishing.

Along with the usual tasks of a Deputy Head, one of Heather's immediate challenges was to integrate her Kenilworth staff and girls into Princethorpe life. She always thought that this went remarkably smoothly. She always enjoyed teaching at Princethorpe and would return home most evenings with many a heart-warming story to share. In particular, she appreciated being able to team up with so many friendly and cooperative members of staff, notably Fathers Alan Whelan and Teddy O'Brien MSC, Marie-Louise O'Keeffe and Sue Millest. She worked well with John Shinkwin, who became a lifelong family friend, as well as with Ed Hester, who succeeded John Shinkwin as Head in 2009.

Her many contributions to college life were noted and appreciated in a publication of 2016 marking fifty years' achievements of Princethorpe College. "Heather played a significant role in patient negotiations over many months, resulting in the creation of the Princethorpe Foundation ... [the Foundation comprises three schools: Princethorpe, Crackley Hall and The Crescent School in Bilton]. Her warm-heartedness and gentle, caring, selfless personality had a great impact ... She loved her Religious Studies teaching as her profound faith was the bedrock of her life."[4]

Heather had returned to teaching in 1994 and continued on and off until 2010. This period coincided with a sharp increase in the number of teachers and trainee teachers who enrolled with Life Light in order to acquire their CCRS qualification enabling them to teach in a Catholic school. The annual updating of our four CCRS modules which related to primary and secondary school practice benefited greatly from Heather's ongoing input. Just as, after we got married, she helped to maintain a series of texts which could be read comfortably by our female students, so now she helped to make them readable by teachers.

Farewell to Oxfordshire

Heather's new post meant that we had to move house to be nearer her place of work. Leaving our beloved Milton-under-Wychwood was emotionally difficult for us. Heather and I had fond memories of our twenty-five years spent in our little Oxfordshire Cotswold village. Phil was reluctant to leave his mates. Liz, still at Oxford Brookes, had already flown the nest. We looked over two properties. I preferred one in Claydon, Oxfordshire; Heather preferred one in Napton-on-the-Hill, Warwickshire. We moved into Napton in September 2002!

"Windward, Vicarage Road, Napton-on-the Hill" is an address very familiar to thousands of our Life Light students. This was the most spacious accommodation Life Light had enjoyed up to that point. It had pleasant views to the east and was situated in a thriving and friendly ancient Warwickshire village dating back to Doomsday. Napton forms part of the Catholic parish of St Wulfstan in Southam. However, Heather and I found it more convenient to use St Anne's in Wappenbury and the beautiful college chapel in Princethorpe.

Phil, now twenty-three, quickly established himself in his new address. After a number of short-term employments, he set up Titan Installation Services. He met and married Amy Morgan in June 2007. Heather always maintained that Amy was "the best thing that had happened to our family in years". She also modestly maintained that Amy was a better mother than she had ever been: Joshua arrived in January 2009. Liz, meantime, having graduated with honours in History of Art from Oxford Brookes University, worked for a number of years in estate agency in and around Oxford.

The first decade of the new millennium was indeed a period of *paradisus domesticus*. We had previously worked out a lay spirituality: we now tried to put it into practice. For the most part this brought a deep peace which I think even St Bernard of Clairvaux would have recognized! But this tranquillity was about to be tested . . .

12

Tranquillity Tested and Restored

A memorable holiday

It started off, as in previous years, as just another summer holiday: we would agree a destination, I would do the detailed planning and off we would go. That year, 2010, I wanted to tour Spain (to complete our European series of holidays), Heather wanted to tour the Outer Hebrides (she had always wanted to visit Iona)—so off we went to Scotland. Truth to tell, we had other reasons for not leaving the UK that year. Amy and Phil had welcomed Lauren into their family in June. Grandma Heather wanted to be on hand!

As usual we left the car at home. We treated ourselves to a "Freedom of Scotland" ticket which covered trains, boats and some coaches—ideal for car-free island hopping. We took in the Edinburgh Festival, we luxuriated in the most scenic railway line in Scotland (Glasgow-Oban-Fort William), and our inter-island ferry trips on Caledonian-McBrayne produced an enormous number of pictures. We toured the Isle of Harris, returning through Skye, the Kyle of Lochalsh and Inverness. We even managed to take in a return visit to our honeymoon hotel at Loch Duich in Dornie.

But it was Iona Abbey that engaged us the most. We spent a whole weekend on the island. Daniel O'Leary had introduced us to Celtic spirituality. Heather always appreciated the closeness of God in Celtic spirituality mediated by the ordinary experiences of daily living: wind, travel, rain, sunshine and light—the presence of God felt through creation. We had to buy extra bags to convey home all the books, leaflets, art and other objects that caught her imagination.

On the last lap of our journey between Inverness and Napton, Heather began to feel a sore throat. Her doctor later assured her that it would pass.

However, a subsequent CT scan revealed cancer of the oesophagus. A fortnight later she was admitted to Coventry University Hospital and began chemotherapy which lasted over Christmas 2010. The operation to remove the cancer was unsuccessful.

Heather died peacefully on 13 May 2011 in Myton Hospice in Warwick, surrounded by all her family, including her mother, Noreen. Father Teddy O'Brien attended her frequently during her last days and administered the last rites. He was also present at the moment of her death.

A selfless personality

Throughout her adult life Heather was always an outward-looking person. She routinely put the other person first and responded actively and promptly to any kind of need if it was in her power to do so. Her "selfless personality" was recorded, as we have seen, while she was at Princethorpe. Her last days were no different. It was as if she had coolly resolved, on hearing the news that her condition was terminal, to "do a good job on dying". She confided to me that she wanted to cause as little inconvenience as possible by her death. I and the family were to grieve her passing—but then get on with our lives as smoothly as possible.

I have a letter written by her to Ed Hester, Head of Princethorpe, in March 2011. In it she offers her resignation from the College. She timed the letter with an eye to the academic cycle, to enable a replacement to be advertised in good time for the 2011–12 academic year. She responded to the tsunami of cards, emails, calls, prayers, flowers and visits, both from individual members of staff and from the College community as a whole. She generated a wish-list of items that I was to see to regarding Noreen's welfare, the education of her grandchildren Josh and Lauren, and much else. I have a small notebook in which she had composed messages to various members of the family. These included birthday card messages to Josh and Lauren, for use after her death. There was even an insert into my own wedding speech for use at Liz's wedding! At the time, Liz was not even engaged, but Heather recognized a future spouse in Mick Messer, even though he and Liz were not to tie the knot for another couple of years.

Her Requiem Mass was concelebrated by Father Teddy O'Brien, Father Alan Whelan and my brother Tony on 21 May in the College chapel at Princethorpe. It had been meticulously planned and lovingly executed by the staff, choir and students, despite the fact that all were heavily involved in summer examinations. Former Head John Shinkwin delivered a touching eulogy. The College staff provided a guard of honour after the Mass. The catering staff laid on an excellent and very generous buffet in the Sixth Form Centre. A bench and plaque were later installed in memory of Heather in the College quad.

Coping with bereavement and grief

"Grieve, and then get on with life." Always difficult! At Lumen Vitae, I wrote an essay on bereavement grief and its pastoral care. In it, I recorded my own conclusions regarding the need to grieve. It is a stage in bereavement that should not be omitted. My own "stiff upper lip" approach to life made me omit it following Uncle Chris' untimely death in 1966—and I lost my voice for a week.

So this time I unashamedly cried. Often. I would be driving during that summer of 2011. My radio would play a piece of classical music that Heather and I had shared and loved. I would have to pull over, park . . . and cry. I cried with others too—mostly Noreen. She had now lost her only child, her only daughter. I felt that part of my own responsibilities was to support Noreen through her own poignant bereavement grief, sharing together the recollected memories of Heather, the might-have-beens, should-have-beens, should-not-have-beens, irrationalities, ups and downs, mood swings. She would ask: "Where is she?" I most often replied "She is with Harry" (Noreen's husband and Heather's father who had died in 1978).

I often reflect upon Noreen's question in the context of my own personal experience. In a sense, Heather has never left me. The settings she entered into the washing machine—I still use them. The material things we shared together—plates, cutlery, furniture, garden tools, etc.—mediate her presence. Similarly with the immaterial things we shared: certain pieces of music torpedo my spirit whenever they reach my ears. When I go to Mass, we still go together. When I pray, I feel that the presence of God is somehow intermingled with the presence of Heather.

Our human experience of God, as also of life, has a transcendent element and an immanent element. I have described how I came to contemplate that transcendent element in terms of time and history. Heather has passed into that history—that history of God who has over billions of years energized our ongoing evolution. In a real sense she is a moment in God's story. She has contributed to both the being and wellbeing of God's creation. She has passed into the transcendent. "Life is changed, not ended." (Preface of funeral Masses.)

She is with God.

The family experienced a new closeness over this testing period. This was very therapeutic. Phil especially was a tower of strength, keeping his own feet on the ground—and ours too. In our frequent get-togethers, we would remind ourselves of Heather's last wishes—especially that we should get on with our lives.

Noreen moved from Barton-on-Sea to nearby Southam, to be nearer the family. "Windward" was now too large for a single occupant, so I downsized to the nearby village of Stockton, enabling Amy, Phil, Josh and Lauren to make a new home in Windward. Liz and Mick got married in 2013; Lilly was born in 2015 and Alice in 2019.

Life Light's future in doubt

Heather's wish was granted: we were all getting on with our lives. This included, of course, my own running of Life Light. Enrolments continued at a steady flow, course material production went on as smoothly as ever, tutoring continued thanks to the tireless devotion of Peter McCafferty, Susan Kowal and Alan Geary. Certificates were promptly issued by Rebecca Hayward of the Board of Studies of the Bishops' Conference. Board meetings were held regularly, and I never missed one. Then, in the summer of 2014, I was diagnosed with cancer of the colon.

Heather and I often joked that if one of us developed a pain anywhere, a corresponding pain would (if anatomically possible!) occur in the other. Sore throats were easily explained, male discomfort during pregnancy is a well-documented phenomenon. But in our case, if *she* got a pain in her left shin, I would be rubbing my left shin the following day. Cancer develops at different rates in accordance with where it occurs. It grows quickly in the oesophagus and slowly in the colon. I calculated that our two cancers had started around the same time. We were running true to form!

The diagnosis gave rise to grave problems regarding the future of Life Light. I had not made any arrangements for Life Light in the event of my own death. For too long I had kept the administration as simple as possible. While this policy made sense over the early years, it seemed as if it might be backfiring now.

I broke the news of my cancer to the family. Liz offered to help. She and Phil had grown up with Life Light from their earliest childhoods. Liz offered to do a crash course on how to run things and to cover for me during my treatment. Having left estate agency work, she had been engaged in human resources work for a period of time. Around the time of my diagnosis, she was beginning to tire of this work, so the prospect of becoming her own boss, aged thirty-three, did not lack a certain appeal. She quickly mastered the Life Light procedures.

A few weeks after my diagnosis, I was admitted to Warwick Hospital, where my cancer was successfully removed. It was a textbook operation. I was back home in three days and marking my essays again in five. Five years later, in August 2019, I was given the "all clear". I owe my life to the NHS and to Warwick Hospital in particular.

Liz quickly settled into her new job and found it quite fulfilling. The future of Life Light began to look clearer. Later, when Liz went on maternity leave, Amy offered cover. With enrolments increasing—especially during the COVID-19 pandemic of 2020–1, Amy agreed to continue as administrator, thereby ensuring that Life Light was in a stronger position than ever.

What a wonderful family I have! Heather would be truly delighted with all this.

Tranquillity restored

Heather was only fifty-seven when she died. She was teaching right up until a few months beforehand, and after she had received her diagnosis. Her passing was truly untimely. When we vowed to be faithful to each other "till death do us part" neither of us could have foreseen that this would be how the parting would actually be. There was a nineteen-year age-gap between us. All our domestic arrangements—especially financial ones—were made on the assumption that I would depart this life first. I frequently agonized over the grief that Heather would experience at that point. Now all was changed: in the immediate aftermath of losing Heather, I wondered whether I could ever be really happy again. But I knew that she wanted me to be—and this was my constantly recurring reflection.

Within a short period of time, I grew to appreciate everything that was positive in my life. In his poem "In Memoriam", Tennyson famously shared his experience of losing a close friend in death: "'Tis better to have loved and lost / Than never to have loved at all." Memories, even painful ones, are better than having no memories.

I still had my close and devoted family, my ever-sympathetic extended family, a fulfilling business, my faith . . . Following the received wisdom of successful widowers, I developed and stuck to a daily routine. I brushed up on my cooking skills and began to entertain Phil on a regular basis to supper. (Yes! I do have a caring family.) I came to see preparing healthy meals as a relaxation from marking essays and arranging courses. Perhaps in particular I reflected that downsizing houses had been a good move to make. Maintaining a smaller house and smaller garden provided constant exercise and would prolong active life.

My contact with the ordinary aspects of daily life had once again become closer and more immediate. Living with Heather had made both of us realize that these form part of our spiritual lives. Perform them well and experience a fleeting smile from God. Now I was learning that this applied to living alone as well.

The ultimate compliment was paid by Liz. Arriving once for a short stay, she observed how tidy my home was. She added: "This house tidies itself!" An instance of a "fleeting smile"—mediated this time by my daughter.

Another act of kindness: in October 2018 the Redemptorists celebrated the Diamond Jubilee of Father Michael Creech. At the original ordination ceremony in 1958, Michael and I were ordained to the priesthood together. I was now invited to the celebratory Mass held in St Mary's, Clapham. I was much moved and appreciated greatly the opportunity afforded of renewing a number of contacts with my former confreres.

Tranquillity was restored!

Life Light and COVID-19

In late 2019, a new coronavirus appeared in Wuhan, China. It spread rapidly around the world, reaching the UK sometime in January 2020. The sufferer experienced varying degrees of influenza-style discomfort, depending mainly upon age, with the elderly being most seriously and often mortally affected. To halt transmission of the virus whole areas were subjected to lockdown. The virus proved more infectious than many previous viruses, especially as it quickly mutated.

As we have seen, the Catholic Certificate in Religious Studies was mostly delivered face to face in university and diocesan centres. These were now ordered to close and their delivery of the CCRS was therefore interrupted.

The Life Light CCRS programme, however, since it is based on distance learning, was able to continue as usual. Furthermore, since we could offer flexible enrolment, it was a much-appreciated facility that a CCRS course participant suddenly facing interruption could immediately transfer to Life Light. In each case, Amy would then design a tailor-made course of study covering the modules needed to complete the particular CCRS course. The success of this system was due in large measure to Amy's hard work and dedication. (She had to oversee her two children's school homeworking during this period as well.)

It is also to the credit of the Board of Studies, which from 1991 had set up and maintained a single CCRS curriculum with agreed standards and quality control, that now hundreds of transfers were thus able to be made smoothly and with a minimum of fuss, and that hundreds of courses were able to be completed despite nationwide dislocation.

13

Sharing a Resource

The year-long period of lockdown and self-isolation provided a unique opportunity to put some order into the letters, files, documents and other bits of paper which had accumulated during the Life Light years. The experience of doing this made me wonder whether I was dealing with a valuable resource—a lifetime of reflection upon deep matters, together with years of reactions from course participants and contributions to a series of issues and debates. Life has taught me much. I have come to a number of conclusions. Some of these, I feel, have a relevance not only to the future of Life Light but more broadly to how we might come to view features of our lives as Christians, the way we might think of God, our spirituality, the functioning of the Church. This chapter endeavours to share some of this resource.

The point in time at which I was engaged upon this exercise coincided with an important initiative taken by Pope Francis. In launching the 2022–3 Roman Synod on synodality, he invited all church members to make their own personal input into how the Church might look in the future. He put a particular emphasis upon listening—the Roman Synod listening to the People of God, and the individual members of the People of God listening to one another.

So here are some thoughts on what Christianity might look like in the future. They are based on my lifelong experience and the insights of thousands of Life Light course participants whom I have had the honour to serve, and are offered here as a possible stimulus to the reader to make their own contribution to the synodical process. I have placed these reflections under the headings of the issues which have most concerned Heather and me as described in this book: God, lay spirituality, the Church, Christian unity.

How can we think about God?

As you are aware, I agonized over God's existence and how to speak to the modern adult about God. This is how I see things at the moment. This is what I would now say to a person who asked for help.

I am aware that I exist. And that I am part of all that is—in time and in space. Part of my awareness takes the form of a question which I simply have to raise. "*Why* is there anything at all?" An eternal chain of cause-and-effect? An originating cause, not itself caused?

When we ask ourselves the question "Why does anything exist at all?" I would suggest that to assert that there was indeed a point when it all began is more rational than any other hypothesis to date. Research into evolution has provided us with compelling evidence of *how* life, once initiated, has developed over aeons of time. It does not pretend to make compelling assertions about any point of initiation.

"Why is there anything at all?" The answer fills me with awe—both at the immensity of cosmic space and time, and the consequential grandeur of its initiation.

For me as a Christian, that awareness of "awe" is transformed into an awareness of "love". The gospel records Jesus as inviting us to react to "the answer to our question" in the way a new baby reacts to a parent—with a loving baby noise, "Abba". (The cosmos is friendly!) Love is *the* most significant environmental factor in the raising of infants into young adults.

We can take love for granted, like the air we breathe. Take air away, life is annihilated. Take love away and life is dramatically changed. Just imagine! New babies would face a wholly different environment (that is, if they managed to be born in the first place). Lifelong wedded bliss would be quite a logical challenge. Dating agencies would rely even more upon vital statistics. Interpersonal relationships would take on the appearance of contractual arrangements. Marriage itself would be reduced to being a mere contract. Cash would replace cuddles. Invoices would replace love letters. Public spirit, national pride, community bonding would fade like the morning mist.

We simply have to affirm and respect universal love if we are to live normal, sustainable lives. Love energizes my living, inspires me to selflessness, enriches my care for my neighbour, suggests meaning to life. Love "makes the world go round". It has in a multiplicity of different ways played a role in evolution. At the heart of Jesus' gospel message is a plea for love—for God and neighbour. That makes perfect sense!

I agonized about God for decades, as I have indicated. As for most children of my age group, God was a man with a white beard who dwelt in heaven just above the clouds. As I grew up, this picture faded from my imagination, although God remained a Supreme Being who was "out there", just beyond the farthest extremities of space. My teachers told me that the existence of this Supreme Being could be proved with certainty from reason.[1] But I had problems with the proofs on offer; it seemed to me that they only worked if you already believed in God's existence.

While I was preparing my thesis at Lumen Vitae, I realized that, in searching after scientific certainty, I had been looking in the wrong direction. Let me explain.

People have their favourite pieces of music. During most of my adult life my whole body has tingled with emotional response to Rachmaninoff's *Second Piano Concerto*. I cannot explain this reaction. Nor do I try to. In my own case anyway, I have no need to subject it to musicological analysis as a condition for my enjoyment. For me, that would be looking in the wrong direction. For me, Rachmaninoff's masterpiece is a "given"—simply to be enjoyed.

Similarly, the air I breathe is a "given". I do not have to prove its existence in order to make use of it, or know that it is composed of oxygen, nitrogen, argon, neon, helium, xenon and krypton. I do not need this information in order to breathe properly. Air is a "given" to be breathed.

And it is the same with humankind's experience of God. It seems that as soon as we evolved into consciousness of our environment, we became aware of something/someone greater than us that directed important features of our lives like climate, crops, death and destiny. From the earliest times of ancestor worship through the major world faiths of the intervening centuries, all have borne witness to variations of this awareness. It has not gone away. The popularity of pieces of music like J. M. Barry's "The Beyondness of Things" are witness to this. Contemplation of the immensity of time and space will always fill us with awe.

In one of the Life Light modules, course participants are invited to reflect upon any personal experience of the presence of God they may have had. They also have the opportunity to share this in a short essay, if they wish—and with not the slightest pressure to do so. Over the years, but increasingly latterly, hundreds have taken up this offer.

Many make the link between their experience of God and storms, mountains, rivers, sunshine, the processes of nature (notably giving birth). "Close to Nature, close to God" is evident in very many offerings. These experiences have taken many different forms—on pilgrimage, at shrines, during charitable projects—but there is one frequently recurring pattern. God's presence is felt, sometimes quite vividly, as a comfort and a support at a point in life when the "road ahead" was thick with fog—following bereavement, in face of examinations, a break-up in a relationship. As a result of the experience, the writer discovers the faith and strength to plod on through the fog to better and brighter times. In retrospect, the writers link their experience of God with the subsequent lap of life's journey.

For over half a century, the Alistair Hardy Research Centre in Oxford has been scientifically studying the phenomena of religious experience. David Hay, once the Director of the Centre, sums up the overall findings. He writes: "We now have fairly convincing evidence that [religious or transcendent experience in contemporary Western society] is widespread and that, in a word, it is normal."[2] Nietzsche, Marx and Sartre would find this discomfiting. Surely faith should have died by now!

Therefore, awareness of the transcendent is also a "given".

Up to the point when I was writing my thesis, I had focused on the famous five proofs of St Thomas Aquinas for the existence of God. In so doing, I had in effect tried to start on my journey into God by listening at the feet of Plato and Aristotle, whose proofs Aquinas had christened. I had been looking in the wrong direction, starting my journey from the wrong departure point.

So, as a Christian, I now moved to the feet of Jesus. He told me that "No one comes to the Father except through me" (John 14:6). So how would the human Jesus have experienced God? As a Jew, of course—sensitive to the *presence* of the God of Life in creation and throughout Jewish history. In other words, as a "given".

Living in the presence of God

This is how I discovered that God was not a reality to be proved but rather a Presence to be experienced. When I open my mind and heart to the presence of God, everything in my life appears as ultimately something *given*—nature, family, friends, neighbours, society, possessions—it has all come into my consciousness through a long history of evolution watched over by a Creator God. An item that I might have regarded as "mine" (because I bought it) I now share with the ultimate Giver. And it is shared with love, a two-way love.

When I open my heart and mind to God's presence in this way, the natural world, my family, friends, neighbours, society, possessions, all take on a friendly glow—as when the sun breaks out over the city and all life and buildings are immediately transformed. When I live in God's presence, though, the glow is always there. The sun will eventually go down on the city: the presence of God is 24/7.

We must once again make it cool to walk in the presence of God. His presence is a source of strength in difficulty, an immediate help in need, and a deeper level of fulfilment in moments of joy. He is as close to us as we are to ourselves. However, to experience God we have to learn to activate our receptors. The most earth-moving concert may be being broadcast as I walk through the fields, but unless my headphones are switched on I hear nothing, despite the radio waves all around me. In a similar way, if I live my life in the presence of God, he communicates to me through all that is around me—flowers, trees, fellow humans. He gives me a hug when I help a neighbour in need. Making contact is as easy and immediate as internally talking to ourselves: prayer is as natural as breathing.

Such living does not call for special clothes or a solemn face. It is our normal everyday life, with all its happenings, successes, fulfilments and failures, but experienced at a deeper level and within the broader horizons of life.

Jesus revealed the presence of God not only in himself but in all of us. This is the immanent dimension of our experience of God, as distinct from the transcendent dimension—the awareness that God is beyond the limits of our knowledge. The transcendental dimension, which was for centuries approached in terms of metaphysics, I now understand in terms of time and history—in keeping with the thinking of the Hebrew scriptures and therefore of Jesus.

God as life itself

I indicated in Chapter 7 that this transcendental/immanent structure of our experience of God is relatable to our experience of life itself. Life is immanent to each one of us as an individual: life also transcends us, and (in its totality) is beyond us in time and space. Life is as old as time itself and as immense as the universe. The Hebrew scriptures are prefaced (cf. Genesis 1) with a dramatic proclamation that God is the "God of Life"—the most basic of all the titles that the Hebrew scriptures gave to God. Life is all around us and within us. "Once we equate God with life itself, a transformation takes place in the way we believe."[3]

Living the full reality

In the introduction to his last book, published posthumously, Daniel O'Leary offers a thought-provoking piece of speculation. "When the planets have all been charted and occupied . . . and the full story of a trillion years of creation is spoken out for the first time, it will be finally clear that all growing is God's growing, that all healing is God's healing, that every age was an age of love."[4] That "full story" will include the saga of humankind's emerging out of Africa some 70,000 years ago, our slow but sure spread over every part of planet earth and our current efforts to make homes on other planets. I cannot contemplate this story in any other way than as being God's own story, or account for it in isolation from God's creativity and support.

As a Christian, I have come to experience the presence of God as an ever-present part of my life. I can relate through God to the entirety of life's story and to its future evolution. I can find joy, peace and fulfilment in being content to be a microscopically small individual in the enormous *complexus* of ongoing cosmic life. I can show my wholehearted love of God by cooperating with what I can glimpse of God's project for humanity—as a way of complying with the first of Jesus' two great commandments. And, as regards the second one, I will love my neighbour as myself to help bring about the reign of God in our time.

We often refer to our need to "live in the real world". When we do so, we are affirming this to be a positive attitude to life. The present need is for us to broaden our horizons and to start living in the real *universe*, with its past history, present challenges and future prospects. Only then will we be able to judge the issues of our age in a more realistic light—not only nuclear weapons, saving our planet, international relations, space research and so on, but also all expressions of personal selfishness, greed, inequality of opportunity, discrimination and racial prejudice. Only then will we be able to make sense of heroism, selflessness and dedication to projects that only become fruitful after our death—no longer "What's in it for me?" but rather "What's in it for all of us?"

To people of faith, this mindset is natural. A self-opening to God in prayer is communication with One who was from "the beginning, is now and ever shall be". Talking to God about a present problem immediately places it in an eternal context, possibly reduces its enormity and/or suggests a long-term solution. Almost always this practice reduces stress.

A faith mindset makes living in the real universe a more fulfilling experience. We may not know what the meaning of life is, but with a mindset of faith we can live lives which are somehow in tune with it—and therefore more meaningful, joyful and peaceful.

This is how I now speak to the modern adult about God.

Marriage matters

If we think of God in terms of life, this has repercussions for the way we think of marriage and its spiritual dimensions. Heather and I devoted much time to producing a spirituality of marriage. Here are some practical implications.

Firstly, we would do well to re-examine our current attitudes to marriage. These have been subjected to a number of philosophical trends, pressure groups and other influences. Notable among these is Marxism.

Karl Marx (1818–83) prophesied in the *Communist Manifesto* of 1848 that class struggle would lead to the downfall of the Western democracies. When this did not happen, some neo-Marxists, aided by postmodernist subjectivism, substituted *cultural* struggle for the failed class warfare. One of their targets was traditional marriage and the nuclear family, perceived as a major component of an undesirable power structure. In *The Origins of the Family, Private Property and the State* (1884), Friedrich Engels (1820–95) had argued that traditional marriage and the family perpetuated social class structures by allowing the transfer of private property through inheritance. Since the mid-twentieth century these and other influences have had the effect of downgrading marriage. (I am indebted to Matthew Gibbs, a course participant, for providing input into this paragraph.)

For millennia, matrimony has been identified by two principal characteristics: (1) mutual love, and (2) children. The word itself, "matrimony", derives from the Latin *matris* and *munus* (the role of the mother)—thereby indicating that society had children in mind even as the loving couple were pronouncing their vows!

Over the last half century the second characteristic has been progressively eclipsed by the first. Children have been de-emphasized. The focus is currently on the mutual love of the contracting parties. This enabled the extension of the concept of marriage to include same-sex couples. This brought about a further change: husbands and wives came (well-meaningly) to be called "partners", a term which was inclusive of same-sex couples.

"Partners" is used also to refer to unmarried couples. More and more young people are choosing not to go through all the bother of a wedding. In the UK between 1981 and 2012, the total annual number of marriages fell by 39 per cent. Couples who marry are more likely to stay together for a longer period of time than cohabiters. This in itself would indicate that society should promote marriage: when couples split, the taxpayer often (though not by any means always) picks up the bill for childcare, single-parent family benefits, homelessness and ill-health.

How can the state help? First, there should never be any tax penalties for getting married. It should never be tax-disadvantageous to get married. Without unduly discomforting the unmarried, it should be possible to order tax regimes that are sensitive to society's need to encourage stable homes in which the next generation of citizens may be raised. The long-term benefits to society, not to mention to the Exchequer, will be appreciable.

The churches too have a role to play here. Traditionally they make, maintain and mend marriages—and do so from a solid base of pastoral experience. However, I frequently read essays which tell of young friends who would love to get married but who cannot for a number of reasons. These are mostly financial, but sometimes there are family pressures to marry in church which cannot easily be accommodated. Sometimes one member of the couple is unchurched, or belongs to a different denomination, or has not been to church since leaving school and so on. In my own experience, priests and clergy go out of their way to be welcoming and understanding of these and many other situations—that is, if ever they get the chance.

When Heather and I were working on *Marriage Today*, Ian Calvert shared with us a piece of Church legislation which gave any person living within the parish boundaries the right to be married in the parish church. This got us thinking.

Many young couples today cannot get married because they cannot afford to. Torn between putting their savings towards their first house deposit or towards a wedding, they feel bound to choose the deposit. Weddings are expensive. They are becoming even more so as wedding venues become ever more lavish and offer licensed premises for the marriage itself, thereby offering the facility of exchanging vows and celebrating afterwards within a single setting.

A suggestion: could not our parish churches enter into competition with the lavish wedding venues? They can offer a well tried-and-tested setting for weddings—the church itself!—more spacious, appropriate, architecturally fitting, and certainly more photogenic than most venues. If a parish church has a suitable parish hall, a modest investment could probably make it suitable for a pleasing wedding reception. Caterers could be brought in for each occasion. Alternatively, with a little long-term planning, a team of motivated parishioners could receive training to do this in-house.

Intending couples could be offered a package deal comprising facilities for the celebration of their marriage and the wedding reception afterwards. The charge would have to cover all the expenses involved in providing this package as well as a contribution to church funds. It would be difficult for the resultant figure not to be competitive!

According to the Office for National Statistics, the number of marriages celebrated in Church of England churches fell 104 per cent between 1981 and 2012. In Catholic churches, the figure was 209 per cent. My suggestion might be a way of reversing this trend. It could also provide a meaningful and realistic contact point with the unchurched. If my Chapter 8 demonstrates anything, it should be to show that objectively the Transcendent is involved in the loving coming together of two people in marriage—whether they believe in God or not. The prenuptial sessions could provide an opportunity to open their eyes to the broader dimensions of what they are about to enter into together.

The "package" need not be restricted to exchanging vows and feasting afterwards. Contact with the parish team would introduce the couple to a community of support through the early years of their marriage, facilitate christening(s), entry to faith schools, and doubtless much else.

We need a multi-pronged approach to promote a fresh vision of marriage, with all the benefits to society which that would enable. This will require change—in particular on the part of the Catholic Church, which we shall now address.

Towards a married clergy

I served as a priest for sixteen years. During that time, I frequently found myself speaking to individuals, groups and whole church congregations about human love and marriage. For many years following the proclamation of *Humanae vitae* in 1968 I was required to explain as helpfully as possible this encyclical which, among other things, outlawed any act of sexual intercourse which was not open to the possibility of conception. I recall that the faces of my listeners communicated back to me a plethora of messages—sympathy, gratitude, enlightenment, pity—which were often translated into words of respectful incredulity. In terms of promoting marriage, the celibate communicator—whether a priest or not—speaks at a disadvantage. It would really assist this important aspect of the Church's ministry if more of the Catholic clergy were married. (At the time of writing, in the Catholic Church only permanent deacons may be married.) The permanent presence of the presbytery home within a parish could offer a constant visual aid of Christian marriage.

In Chapter 4, I referred to living through the 1971 Synod of Rome which reaffirmed the traditional discipline of celibacy. I have long thought that the traditional shape of the Catholic priesthood—restricted to baptized celibate males—needs to change. There are many reasons why such a change is necessary and they have been widely and intensively researched and discussed over the half century since the 1971 Roman Synod. In response to an essay title on "Priestless parishes—what should be done?", those course participants who select this topic manifest an overwhelming consensus: make celibacy optional. They also want ordination to be open to women, although most realistically think that the issue of celibacy should be dealt with first.

Was Jesus married?

I feel that the Catholic Church is close to making this change. When it does so, I will wager that we shall hear more about the marital status of Jesus—always a crucial issue whenever celibacy is discussed. While Heather and I were working on our Theology of Marriage module, we researched this point. Our findings were never incorporated into the text of our module: we realized at the time that even raising the possibility of Jesus being married would cause distress. However, if mandatory priestly celibacy is indeed close to being abolished, perhaps now would be an opportune time to share what we discovered.

For nineteen centuries, we have assumed that Jesus was celibate. It is only recently that scholars have begun to question this assumption.[5] Of course, we shall never know for sure. We are dealing with only circumstantial evidence. The circumstantial evidence in favour of Jesus' celibacy has traditionally been based on Mark 2:19 (Jesus' bride was the Church); Luke 14:26 and 20:34–6; also Matthew 19:12 (celibacy as a prerequisite for discipleship—Jesus must have practised what he preached).

The circumstantial evidence in favour of Jesus having been married lies mainly in the fact of his Jewish background. Celibacy was not esteemed throughout the period of the Hebrew scriptures: in fact, not being married was regarded as a sign of God's displeasure. The Hebrew marital customs of Jesus' time and place are well known. They included the arranged marriage: Joseph like all other Jewish fathers would have "married off" Jesus very soon after puberty, if he had not already found someone himself. Had Joseph failed to do this he would have been deemed by Jewish society to have seriously failed in his duty to the Law—whereas Matthew 1:19 calls Joseph "just".

Further, scholars are for the most part agreed that Jesus was a Rabbi. This is relevant here. Even the most revered of the Hebrew religious "hierarchy" were married. Leviticus 21:13ff. indicates that the High Priest himself is a married man. Similarly, the Nazarite, who took many vows, was never required to take a vow of celibacy (cf. Numbers 6). On the contrary, human love, marriage, love-making and especially having children were regarded as pertaining to the very heart of Hebrew spiritual life. Being unmarried was regarded as a sign of the curse of God: for example, Jephthah's daughter "bewails her virginity" in Judges 11:37. In classical Hebrew, there was no word for "bachelor"; clearly there were not too many of them around!

It was a strong point of the teaching of the Rabbis that all should marry. "Marriage was regarded not only as the normal state, but as a divine ordinance."[6] G. F. Moore records that in the second century AD, there was one Rabbi who apparently, and very exceptionally, was not married and who was taken to task for not practising what he preached. So the conclusion may reasonably be made that, since most Rabbis *did* practise what they preached, Rabbis like all Hebrew males were expected to marry and did so. This seems to have been the case throughout the period of the Hebrew scriptures and into the first centuries of the Christian era.

The Gospel texts have no explicit reference to Jesus getting married, or to Jesus not getting married. Given the background, the latter would have been the more remarkable of the two possibilities. The silence of the Gospels about Jesus' marriage is therefore really a factor in support of Jesus having been married. Certain passages in the New Testament make it less likely that there was a tradition about Jesus' celibacy at the time of their composition: for example, Philippians 2:7 refers to Jesus as "being *in every way* like a human being"; and Hebrews 2:17: "It was essential that he should in this way be made *completely* like his brothers."

If Jesus was indeed married, who was his wife? It seems that there is only one candidate—Mary Magdalen.[7] The second-century *Gospel of Philip*, an apocryphal text discovered in Egypt in 1945, refers to Mary Magdalen as Jesus' partner and spouse,[8] and this close relationship is assumed throughout the second-century *Gospel of Mary* and the third-century *Pistis Sophia*, both discovered in 1896, as well as in other apocryphal texts.

After Jesus' crucifixion all three synoptic Gospels make mention of certain women "who had followed Jesus from Galilee" (Luke 23:55), buying and preparing spices with a view to anointing Jesus' body. Matthew, Mark and Luke differ in the identification of these women. However, Mary Magdalen features in all three lists and always appears in first place. In John's Gospel, she is the only woman mentioned in this context. Dame Rabbi Julia Neuberger gave a *Thought for the Day* on BBC Radio, during which she alluded to this anointing of Jesus. She made the observation that, in the context of first-century Jewish practice, the woman who brought spices to anoint Jesus' dead body *had* to be his wife. It was strictly forbidden for any other woman to perform this service.

The silence of the Gospels is possibly an indication that Jesus' marital status was the same as everybody else's. Given the context—first-century Judea—it would be presumed that he was indeed married. The earliest reference we have to the idea that Jesus was *not* married is in the writings of Tatian (c. AD 110–72), *On Perfection according to the Saviour*, written about a century after Jesus' resurrection. Tatian was writing during a period when Roman men thought it smart to avoid marriage altogether. The demographic consequences of this practice became so dire that, as we saw in Chapter 8, the Emperor Augustus (63 BC–AD 14) had to pass a law in 18 BC requiring Romans to be married. This law was repealed only in AD 320 by Constantine. Tatian may have been reinterpreting the evidence in favour of his own milieu(?)

The idea that Jesus never married flourished during the early centuries of monasticism, as well as during periods of enforced clerical celibacy. It is commonly assumed to be Church teaching, although the point has never been defined by the Magisterium.

An indication of change

Over the period of the Synod on the Amazon (2019–20), Pope Francis indicated a greater readiness to countenance a change to mandatory celibacy than any of his immediate predecessors. But he was blocked by certain sections of the Roman Curia.

Pope Pius XII found himself in a similar situation in the years after World War II. With the cessation of hostilities, he saw the urgent need for a Council. The Curia would not cooperate. His successor, Pope St John XXIII, found a solution. With no prior warning to the Curia, he simply announced the Second Vatican Council to the Church and world at large. The Curia had no choice but to start preparing for it.

Pope Francis could take a leaf out of John XXIII's book. He could announce to the Church at large that Canon 1037 of the Code of Canon Law need no longer be observed. This is the Canon which requires a candidate for the priesthood to undertake the obligation of celibacy before being admitted to the order of deacon. Alternatively, by omitting three words of the Latin text of Canon 1037 and modifying a fourth, he could make this undertaking optional.

He could then, in line with his publicly expressed ideas on the merits of synodality, indicate that this change would be implemented or not implemented at local level, and not overseen by the Roman Curia. In the first place, the local Bishops' Conferences would consider the changed status of Canon 1037 and initiate discussion forums with a view to discerning the wishes of the faithful.

Very likely, the local churches would not proceed at the same pace: first entrants into seminary of the new type of seminarian would be spread over a number of years. In any case, there would be five or six years of training before any married/marriageable candidates would be considered for ordination. In other words, there would be no sudden change. There would be time for any who opposed this change to be heard and helped respectfully, lovingly and constructively.

A modification of Canon 1037 could also open a way for permanent deacons to be considered as candidates for the ordained priesthood. This would, of course, depend upon the consent of their wives. Such a development would more swiftly ease the shortage of priests which is currently being widely experienced.

For what it is worth, I am convinced that a married Catholic clergy could help solve another problem as well. For decades now, the Catholic priesthood has sadly been beset with many instances of clerical sexual abuse and their cover-up by ecclesiastical superiors. Much progress has been made in addressing this problem and ensuring better practice and safeguards for the future. The Church now needs to draw a line under these scandals. We need to turn the page. The demarcation between the old and the new needs to be credible, visible, clear-cut, unmistakeable. The appearance in our sanctuaries of an ordained priest who is known to be legally married, whose wife is known to the parish community, and whose children attend their own children's school—that could be the clear sign that the Catholic Church has put its past behind it and is indeed making a fresh start.

Tackling Church disunity

During the COVID-19 crisis of 2020–1, several Christian denominations edifyingly came together to address the social needs of their localities. While this earned plaudits from all sides, it also raised consciousness—yet again—of the scandal of our disunity.

Over the past millennium, the Orthodox Churches have separated from the Western Churches, the Churches of the Reformation have separated from the Catholic Church, Non-conformist Churches have separated from the Church of England—the list is embarrassingly long. Why do Churches separate from one another?

Churches rarely split bottom-up—in response to the wishes of the people of God. Just the opposite, in fact: people in the pew tend not to welcome changes. Think, for example, of the Pilgrimage of Grace (1536) and the Devon and Cornish Rebellion (1549).

Churches have mostly split top-bottom—because of disputed points of Church teaching. A few examples. Does the Holy Spirit proceed from the Father *through* the Son (as in the theology of the Orthodox Churches), or from the Father *and* the Son (as in Western theology)? Are we justified by faith alone, *sola fide* (as in Protestantism), or by good works (as in Catholicism)? Do bishops have a place in church government (as in Anglicanism), or not (as in non-conformity)? Of course, there were other issues involved in these sad splits: but they rarely were the concern of the pew occupiers. Most separations have occurred because of issues of orthodoxy—"correct teaching".

Little wonder then that current efforts at reuniting our denominations have set out to arrive at agreed statements on Church teaching and so reverse the causes of past splits. The Anglican-Roman Catholic International Committee (ARCIC) has produced Agreed Statements on the Eucharist, Ministry, Church Government, Salvation and the Role of the Pope, as well as other issues. The persons directly involved in such discussions are individuals who can credibly represent their side, usually clerics. It is not surprising, then, that a large proportion of the issues concern the different aspects of church ministry.

Pope Francis has pointed out that this approach has so far been disappointing in terms of results (that is, actual reuniting). He wondered whether, instead of concentrating in these discussions on the sacrament of Order, we should concentrate on the sacrament of Baptism, our common initiation into Christianity. He has thus set up a signpost pointing to the direction in which ecumenical dialogue might proceed.

What might this signposted road look like? All baptized Christians could be invited to set out on a journey. The departure point is the place where we find ourselves in our here-and-now—in our various denominations, traditions and as inheritors of our past stories. The destination would be a place where each one of us would explicitly and unreservedly recognize each other as fellow followers of Jesus. As we travelled along the road towards our common destination, we would probably have to undergo a series of mindset changes. These would not necessarily involve our denying the realities and details of our traditions and the events of our past stories, but we may have to *reprioritize* them in the interests of the greater good: Christian unity.

Whether the Holy Spirit proceeds from the Father through the Son or from the Father and the Son, a higher priority might be for both of us to work together to get the soup out on time to feed the hungry. This is ortho*praxis* viewed as a higher priority than ortho*doxy*—"good practice", rather than "correct teaching". Both are important, but which is more so? What would Jesus have said about this?

As Christian denominations we have divergent criteria for admission to ministry. Some admit married men and women, others restrict it to celibate men. Could we not find it in our hearts to countenance a unified Christianity which recognized both sets of arrangements, thereby facilitating a more intensely spiritual clerical collaboration at grass roots, nationally and internationally?

There is a Christian precedent for living with seemingly irreconcilable differences. In the late sixteenth century, a theological debate raged unproductively between the Jesuits and the Dominicans regarding the roles of grace and free will in human acts. Pope Clement VIII (1592–1605) intervened. He imposed silence on both sides with the words "*abundet quisquam in sensu suo*" ("let each find fulfilment in their own opinion").

Could we not in our own day apply this piece of wisdom to our own seemingly irreconcilable issues? Let us take a crucial example: eucharistic hospitality. Many denominations welcome all Christians to share Communion. The Catholic Church currently does not—at least not officially.[9] For a number of theological reasons the Catholic Church restricts the reception of Holy Communion to members of the Catholic faith. It values the Eucharist as a sign of unity already achieved, rather than as a means of achieving unity. The question of how the eucharistic miracle—transubstantiation—takes place is also a point of doctrinal divergence. Despite these differences, across the Christian denominations the actual celebration of the Eucharist is clearly meaningful, fulfilling, inspiring and a sincere response to Jesus' invitation to "do this in memory of me".

As we plod along the road towards church unity, could we not become prepared to countenance the different modes of doing this "in memory of me" and rejoice in the fact that we are actually doing it and obeying

Jesus' invitation, and deprioritize the points of irreconcilable differences of the actual mode of celebration? The rewards would be many:

- Inter-church families would be able to join fully in the Eucharist as a family—this would be a great help in the religious education of their children.
- The less mobile and the elderly would be able to find a local church in which to celebrate the Eucharist, in cases where they are no longer capable of travelling to the denomination of their baptism.
- School Masses would become more meaningful and easier to plan if all baptized students could be invited to play their full part in the liturgy. This could contribute notably to developing and maintaining a Christian school ethos.
- Places of pilgrimage would flourish more, and be creative of church unity, if they could offer a single liturgy instead of having to provide multiple liturgies.
- New inter-denominational forms of religious life could more smoothly organize their liturgical lives.[10]
- Regular shared worship could well lead in the long term to a gradual harmonization of liturgical ritual and so promote church unity in a meaningful way.
- Eucharistic hospitality would give local churches an incentive to welcome newcomers more warmly and to provide ever more attractive services.

As we have seen, there have been two traditions in the Catholic Church regarding the signification of the Eucharist. Earlier centuries saw the Eucharist as a sign which was creative of Christian unity. Over the centuries it became a sign of unity already achieved. Those of us who followed developments during Vatican II and afterwards thought that we could discern a return to the earlier tradition. The Missal of St Paul VI (1970) confirmed this in the Eucharistic Prayer after the consecration: "Grant that we, who are nourished by the body and blood of your Son and filled with his Holy Spirit, may become one body, one spirit in Christ."[11] In this formula the words "may become" take account of the possibility that there are some present who do not as yet form "one body, one spirit in Christ". However, the Catechism of the Catholic Church maintains the "unity already achieved" signification of the Eucharist.[12]

Eucharistic hospitality could become possible if, in the spirit of Clement VIII, the different denominations could find fulfilment (*abundet quisquam*) in their various approaches to the Eucharist, offer a welcome to all the baptized and progressively work towards harmonization of our procedures in the long-term future.

Apart from the advantages listed above, this development would give a boost to something that is happening already—the ever-larger degree of inter-church and inter-faith collaboration in favour of the poor and needy in our urban areas. There have been many examples during the COVID crisis of local churches teaming up to provide much-needed groceries and household requirements to destitute families and homeless individuals. In the reordering of priorities, such forms of ministry must come high on our lists.

Orthopraxis before orthodoxy!

Lay spirituality

Having had the rich experience of a quarter of a century of monastic spirituality, followed by half a century of lay spirituality, I have outlined the general features of a lay spirituality that would sit just as comfortably with the realities of lay life as monastic spirituality sits with those of the religious. Here is a summary.

The solid foundation of lay spirituality is the contemplation of the God of Life—in creation, evolution and our future destiny—and an ever-deepening consciousness of our involvement in this process (especially through procreation). Everything in life thus relates to God. Jesus has laid out the priorities of human life: our own personal priorities and those relating to our family and society.

In promoting the being and the wellbeing of life, we daily make microscopically small, but essential, contributions to God's overall designs. We are part of God's story—both in life and in death.

At that point, our life stories become one with God's. Our lives are changed, not ended.

These then are some of the conclusions that I have reached as I have passed through, and reflected upon, the various stages of my life.

What would I now be saying to the hapless occupant of the first house in Land's End?

Probably something very different from what I had in mind as an eight-year-old!

Post-word

I have now told our story, both of Life Light Home Study Courses and our own story. It has been set against a background of rapid change in the Church and in society as a whole. I thank you for your patience as you have accompanied me through my noviciate, seminary, priesthood, laicization, marriage, family life—as well as through my efforts to make a small contribution to adult religious education.

Reasons for optimism

As I come to the end of *Posting the Word*, I am full of optimism for the future of the Catholic Church and Christianity in general.

In the first place, as far as Catholics are concerned, there is Pope Francis' on-going programme of implementation of the Second Vatican Council. For decades, I naively imagined that, in the Vatican, implementation was proceeding cautiously and prudently—as befits a large body of the faithful. The bigger the ship the longer it takes to turn it around! Recently it has become clear that elements in the Vatican Curia have been working to stop the ship from manoeuvring at all. The cardinals that elected Jorge Bergoglio as Pope Francis wanted him to reform the Curia and push forward with Vatican II, especially as regards introducing collegiality into church structures. He is doing this—and far more.

On 10 October 2021, at a large gathering in the Vatican of cardinals, bishops, male and female theologians as well as many others, Pope Francis launched the 2022–3 Roman Synod on synodality. Previously, a Roman Synod was comprised mainly of bishops from around the world who met at intervals to deliberate on issues affecting the whole Church. There was usually little input from interested parties outside the group of bishops. What Francis inaugurated in October 2021 had never been done before in the twenty centuries of Christian history—a Roman Synod which would invite *every* member of the Church to contribute insights and proposals for the life of the Church, with a view to identifying consensus-points in a publicly-available report to be laid before the Pope.

In Chapter 3, I tried to convey something of the joy and enthusiasm of the Vatican II days, with all its hopes and dreams. We could see this joy return if the new synodical process is taken up with any enthusiasm. Vatican II urged everyone to revisit the sources of our faith—"resourcement" was the buzz word at the time—and so renew the way we lived out our Christian faith. Throughout these chapters, I have often wondered aloud and asked "What would Jesus think of this?" when discussing the priorities of Christianity. It is a question we should frequently raise, especially in the context of the Synod.

A further reason for optimism derives from the experience of having lived through the COVID pandemic. When COVID-19 appeared in early 2020, it spread rapidly around the world. It caused disruption to social, educational, commercial and religious life. As everybody sought to combat a common threat, it brought nations and people together. It also made people more sensitive to the deeper issues of life, general wellbeing, and care of the vulnerable. Throughout the UK, we used to stand outside our front doors at 8 pm on Thursday evenings and clap hands to indicate our gratitude to healthcare workers. With churches closed for long periods, there was a new interest in virtual religious services via TV and the internet. Courses in mindfulness were widely advertised. The media reported an increase in the number of people resorting to prayer.

The various lockdowns necessitated by the pandemic gave us time to pull back, reflect and speculate on all our futures. We were forced to become momentarily more dependent upon one another than at any time since the Second World War. This experience could have implications for how we view our lives of faith in a future that is itself threatened by global warming and long-term ecological damage to our planet.

Finally, it may well be that the tide of secularism has turned. In 2019, Michael Symmons Roberts was researching for a radio documentary entitled "A Believer's Guide to Atheism". His research made him increasingly aware that "old-style ridiculing of faith is in sharp decline" and that our world has entered a "post-secular" phase. He also interviewed a number of twenty-year-olds and found open-mindedness in matters of faith.[1]

I discern a general feeling that a purely secularist mindset does not after all interface convincingly with the climatic, ecological, cultural and spiritual challenges that face us, nor with the implications of archaeological findings, nor with space research and the destiny of the human race. Science and faith—for long at loggerheads with each other—could now be converging. Cosmologists reveal ever more mind-boggling facts and figures relating to the dimensions and timescales of the universe. These revelations prompt in us a sense of mystery, awe, fascination and fear of their implications—reactions which interface somewhat with Rudolf Otto's observations in his *Idea of the Holy* concerning humanity's response to the divine.[2]

As I survey the story of Life Light and ponder its future potential, I am especially optimistic. It has been my privilege and honour to have shared the thoughts, hopes, criticisms, fears, joy and frustrations of thousands of (mostly) young adults as they grow in biblical and theological literacy through working through their modules. The essays they presented during lockdown reflected a widespread determination to "make things come right". They and their contemporaries are the hope of the future.

I feel sure that they will not let us down!

APPENDIX 1

List of Modules

in the order in which they were written

The Church
Catholic Theology Since 1800
Introduction to Hermeneutics
The Gospels*
Theology of Religious Life*
The Basics of Christian Believing*
The Church's Liturgy
Christian Morals
Catechetics in the Classroom*
Theology of Marriage
New Testament Greek*
Hebrew Scriptures I
Hebrew Scriptures II
Christian Scriptures I
Christian Scriptures II
Religious Education in the Parish
The Sacraments
The Old Testament
The New Testament
Who is Jesus?
Introduction to Religious Education
RE in the Primary School
RE in the Irish Primary School
RE in the Secondary School

* These modules are not currently on offer

APPENDIX 2

Annual Enrolments, 1974–2021

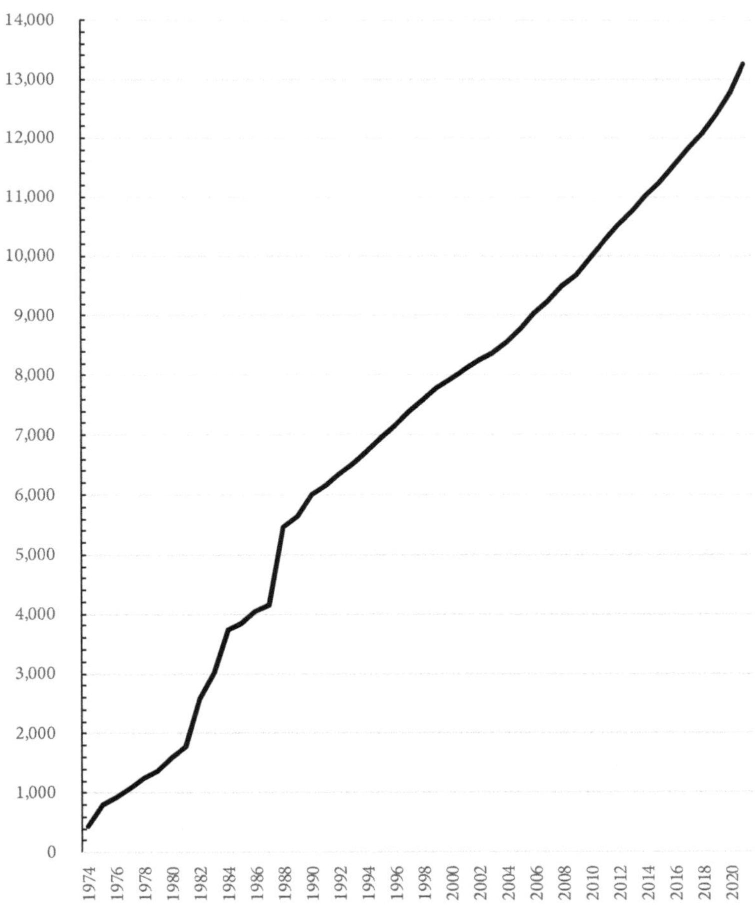

Notes

Chapter 1

1 "The Warsaw Concerto" was composed by Richard Addinsell for the popular morale-boosting film *Dangerous Moonlight* (1941). The famous *Sound of Music* opened on Broadway in 1959.

Chapter 2

1 Cf. Origen (c.184–c.253), *Sermons on the Book of Leviticus 8:3*. He, along with many of his circle, discouraged marking birthdays. This passed widely into monastic practice.

2 E.g. Constitution 285 of the Rules and Constitutions of the Congregation of the Most Holy Redeemer (CSSR).

3 Cf. Stanzas 26–28 of *Ascent of Mount Carmel*. Note that the imagery throughout St John of the Cross' poems is taken from the *Song of Songs* in the Hebrew scriptures. Originally merely joyful wedding pieces, Christian mystics of the Middle Ages freely reinterpreted the texts to make them refer to the loving relationship between God and the individual soul.

4 The English edition, *The Law of Christ*, was published by Mercier Press in 1963.

5 The English edition was published by Sheed and Ward in 1960.

6 The subdiaconate was abolished by Paul VI in 1972.

Chapter 4

1 R. Gryson, *Les origines du célibat ecclésiastique* (Gembloux: Éditions J. Duculot, 1970).

2 *We Celebrate the Eucharist* (Morristown, NJ: Silver Burdett & Ginn, 1984). The Brusselmans programme was widely used around the world. It set the pattern for many other similar programmes which still flourish.

3 ET: London: SCM Press, 1967.

4 Wolfhart Pannenberg, *The Apostles' Creed* (ET: London: SCM Press, 1972).

Chapter 5

1 Founders of the Visitation Sisters, Notre Dame Sisters and the Sisters of Mercy respectively.

2 F. C. Price, a *Catholic Herald* journalist, wrote articles about us in the editions of 26 October 1973; 7 June, 18 and 26 July, 26 October 1974; and 3 January 1975.

3 Cf. 18 October 1974.

4 Cf. edition of 2 November 1973.

5 Pontifical Council for the Instruments of Social Communication, *Pastoral Instruction on the means of social communication*, 29 January 1971. The quotation here is from n. 11.

6 This reference is to *The Cloister and the Hearth*, by Charles Reade (1861), which fictionally contrasts the two settings. (For years I thought that the author was a relative of Father Vincent Reade, Headmaster of St Philip's Grammar School from 1910–37. Hence my fascination!)

Chapter 6

1 *Pastoral Instruction on the means of social communication*, n. 11, a Vatican document of 29 January 1971.

2 Cf. the Life Light module *Who is Jesus?* Unit 3, p. 29.

Chapter 7

1 Cf. R. E. Brown et al., *The New Jerome Biblical Commentary* (London: Geoffrey Chapman, 1989), p. 846; J. Martos, *Doors to the Sacred: A Historical Introduction to the Sacraments of the Church* (London: SCM Press, 1981), p. 176; Life Light Courses, *Christian Scriptures I*, Unit 3, *New Testament*, Unit 2.

2 Cf. *Letter to Lucilius* 41:1.

3 C. Williams, *New Catholic Encyclopaedia*, vol. 4, p. 198.

4 Margaret Sibery, *The Tablet*, 27 May 2019 (italics mine). Cf. also Vatican II, *Gaudium et spes* 22, and St John Paul II, *Donum et vivificantem* 50.

Chapter 8

1 J. P. Dever in *New International Dictionary of the Christian Church*, p. 634. R. Haughton, *Theology of Marriage* (Cork: Mercier Press, 1971), pp. 41ff. and E. Schillebeeckx, *Marriage: Secular Reality and Saving Mystery* (London: Sheed and Ward, 1965), pp. 280ff.

2 Vatican II, *Lumen gentium: Constitution on the Church* 40–1.

3 Ibid. cf. 46–52.

4 For example, Haughton, *Theology of Marriage*, p. 39.

5 Matthew 6:33. Cf. *Lumen gentium* 5.

6 J. V. Taylor, *The Go-Between God* (London: SCM Press, 1972), p. 125.

7 Cf. John Paul II, *Familiaris consortio* 21. Cf. *Catechism of the Catholic Church* 1655–7.

8 Tertullian, *Ad uxorem* 2:9 (quoted in Schillebeeckx, *Marriage*, p. 290).

9 Schillebeeckx, *Marriage*, p. xxviii.

10 Cf. Schillebeeckx, *Marriage*, p. 14.

11 Vatican II, *Gaudium et spes* 48. Cf. *Catechism of the Catholic Church* 1644–5.

Chapter 9

1 *The NEW REview* (Summer 1983), p. 33.

Chapter 10

1 *CCRS: Twenty-Five Years On*, Rejoice Publications, 2019.

Chapter 11

1 Karl Rahner (1904–84). The words were quoted by Christopher Lamb in *The Tablet*, 7 November 2020, p. 28.

2 Etienne Gilson, *The Mystical Theology of St Bernard* (London: Sheed and Ward, 1940). *Paradisus claustralis,* that is, "paradise experienced in the cloister".

3 Noreen is an admirer of Mary O'Hara (b. 1935). She achieved international fame as a singer during the years after she left her Benedictine monastery in Stanbrook Abbey in 1974. She has strong links with Co. Mayo and currently lives on the Aran Islands, just off its coast.

4 Nick Baker and Alex Darkes, *A Spirit of Family: The First Fifty Years of Princethorpe College*, 2016, p. 94.

Chapter 13

1 First Vatican Council, Session 3, Chapter 2. Cf. Denzinger, 1785 / 1806.

2 David Hay, *Religious Experience Today: Studying the Facts* (London: Mowbray, 1990), Preface, p. 1.

3 Daniel O'Leary, *An Astonishing Secret: The Story of Creation and the Wonder of You* (Dublin: Columba Press, 2017), p. 13.

4 Daniel O'Leary, *Horizons of Hope* (Dublin: Columba Press, 2021), p. 21.

5 William Phipps, *Was Jesus Married?* (Washington: University of America Press, 1970) investigates the evidence.

6 G. F. Moore, *Judaism in the First Centuries of the Christian Era*, vol. 2 (Cambridge, MA: Harvard University Press, 2014), p. 119.

7 In 591, Pope Gregory I was the first to link Mary Magdalen with the sinful woman in Luke 7:36–50. Thereafter she was venerated as a penitent sinner. There is no basis in the Gospels themselves for this linkage.

8 *Gospel according to Philip*, Sayings 32 and 55.

9 Austen Ivereigh notes that "Eucharistic hospitality in the Vatican is always more generous than its documents say it should be elsewhere" (cf. *The Tablet*, 6 May 2006).

10 For example, the religious community of young people established by Archbishop Justin Welby within Lambeth Palace. Cf. *The Tablet*, 20 March 2021, pp. 8–9 for an account of this project in which mention is made of this particular problem.

11 Eucharistic Prayer III. Eucharistic Prayers II and IV have similar wording.

12 *Catechism of the Catholic Church* 1398.

Post-word

1 Michael Symmons Roberts, *A Believer's Guide to Atheism*, BBC Sounds documentaries, December 2019. Cf. D. J. Taylor, "Charting Change", *The Tablet*, 13 February 2021, p. 22.

2 Rudolf Otto, *The Idea of the Holy* (Oxford: Oxford University Press, 1923).

Lightning Source UK Ltd.
Milton Keynes UK
UKHW021826280322
400731UK00006B/67